EXPLANATION IN ARCHEOLOGY

An Explicitly Scientific Approach

EXPLANATION
IN ARCHEOLOGY

An Explicitly Scientific Approach

Patty Jo Watson, Steven A. LeBlanc
and Charles L. Redman

COLUMBIA UNIVERSITY PRESS
New York and London

Patty Jo Watson is Associate Professor of Anthropology at Washington University, St. Louis.

Steven A. LeBlanc is Post-Doctoral Fellow in the Department of Human Genetics at the University of Michigan, Ann Arbor.

Charles L. Redman is Assistant Professor of Anthropology at New York University.

" . . . it behooves the archeologist . . . to derive his observational data as objectively as possible, to differentiate between observed fact and derived inference, to make explicitly labeled interpretations of as detailed and full a nature as possible, and then to look, either in the ground or among the data at hand, for evidence by which his hypotheses may be tested . . . above all, let him analyze whatever in fact he does do, so that he may bring into the open the procedures and premises upon which his results are based."

Walter W. Taylor
A Study of Archeology (1948)

PREFACE

MAN HAS ALWAYS sought to understand the world about him. As the fields of science developed, natural laws were incorporated in formalized frameworks or theories for the understanding or explanation of natural phenomena. The formulation and confirmation of such laws and theories is the primary goal of science, that is, the discovery and description not only of what, when, and where, but also of how and why. By use of scientific laws and theories, explanations can be given and predictions made. This is no less true of the newer social sciences than it is of the natural sciences.

A great deal of attention has been given to just what is meant by "explanation" in science and how one achieves it. For a variety of reasons the answers to these questions have not been so straightforward in the social sciences as in the physical sciences. Discussion of this crucial issue continues at the present time, with debate focusing on the question of what constitutes explanation in the social sciences, how social scientists can best achieve it, and whether it is based on laws in such a way that predictions are also possible in the social sciences.

Recently, archeologists have become explicitly concerned with the question of explanation, and while no consensus has yet emerged, there has been so much discussion that it is worthwhile —in fact, necessary—to present a single, coherent synthesis of one possible approach to explanation in archeology. Such a synthesis can serve at least two useful purposes. It can provide an introduction for students to the major theoretical issues in the field, and it can be viewed as a model or trial formulation of a potentially highly productive approach to archeological data.

To begin, we reject the view that anyone is free to choose his own definition of "explanation." Such a procedure would lead only to chaos because without common understandings of words and concepts, investigators cannot build a body of knowledge (see the discussion of classification and typology in Chapter 5, pp. 126–34). We turn to the logical positivist philosophers of science for a carefully considered definition of the word "explanation." To these analytic philosophers, explanation is by no means a vague concept. It means demonstrating that the particular case one wants to explain is an example of general relationships described by an established general law. Such laws are called covering laws, and this type of explanation is called a covering law explanation.

Once this definition is accepted, as we feel it should and will be, a number of very important consequences logically follow. The most obvious and fundamental of these is that to explain anything one must have a body of general laws about the relevant phenomena.

The suggestion that archeologists accept this definition and its consequences has produced a significant amount of controversy over theory among some archeologists, but has left many others unconcerned. To understand why this is the case, we must digress briefly to consider the multiple nature of the broad area of study labeled archeology. Archeology is a term that is widely applied to several rather distinct disciplines or subdisciplines. This is because the word "archeology" is often utilized simply to refer to a set of techniques and methods for the recovery of information about the past that can then be used for various purposes, rather than to refer to a completely independent discipline with a theory, method, and subject matter peculiar to it alone. Further, the separation between anthropological archeology on the one hand, and classical and humanistically oriented archeology on the other, is almost universally accepted. The purposes and objectives of classical archeologists and art historians have traditionally been different from those of archeologists or prehistorians who have been trained in anthropology. It is only the latter archeologists who consider themselves to be primarily social scientists, rather than historians, and it is primarily this group with whom we are concerned. Hence, in this book we are not analyzing humanistically oriented or classical archeology, but anthropological archeology. (It should be noted, however, that to the extent that history is a social science, our conclusions apply to classical archeology as well.)

Within anthropological archeology there has also been somewhat of a division, less fundamental than the one just mentioned. This division follows fairly closely that between archeologists who study the Old World, who are often referred to as prehistorians, and the archeologists who study the New World, who are more closely related to cultural anthropologists than their Old World counterparts. This dichotomy is not of great significance because members of these two subdisciplines are interested in similar problems and have defined similar goals centering on the description and explanation of prehistoric events. While New World archeologists have generated much of the recent concern with explanation, the problem is relevant to both groups, and Old World prehistorians have been quick to enter into serious discussion of this issue.

The understanding of past cultures,[1] and the explanation of the differences and similarities found among them, is generally agreed to be the goal of anthropologically oriented archeology. If we accept this goal and agree on the definition of "explanation"

---

[1] Scientific methods can be applied to archeological data from the entire time range of human evolution. However, a number of validly held assumptions pertaining in later time ranges become hypotheses for testing in the Early and Middle Pleistocene materials: for instance, what kind of patterned behavior can be expected for the earliest hominids, and even whether cultural patterning can be discerned at all.

referred to earlier, then the logical way one must proceed is by the use of the methods of science. In addition, one must discover and follow the logical ramifications of these methods. What it means to be explicitly scientific, or to follow scientific methods, is discussed in the next chapter.

Those archeologists who have been most vocal in urging the adoption of a rigorous definition of "explanation," and in recognizing the need for the confirmation of general laws to be used in explanation, are sometimes called "new archeologists." Some of them are also referred to as processualists or even as progressive archeologists. These terms are charged with ideological connotations, so their descriptive value is obscured. However, much of the difficulty with these words comes from trying to use them to label individual researchers, who do not always hold the position consistently, rather than from any inconsistency in the position itself. If the term "new archeology" is to be used, it should be equated with explicitly scientific archeology, and not be used to refer to the advocates of the position but only to the position itself. Hence, our definition of the phrase "new archeology" is explicitly scientific archeology as defined more fully in Chapter 2.

Although the definition of "scientific explanation" as subsumption of particular cases under general laws is clear and straightforward, the question as to whether to accept and to operate with such a framework is much more difficult. There is an immense literature describing and extolling the virtues of using scientific methods, but the basic reason for adopting them is pragmatic. In practice they provide practical, testable explanations and predictions. It is for this reason that their acceptance within the general framework of scientific archeology is urged.

Yet, adopting a scientific framework as the basis of investigations is only the first step. One must next determine exactly *how* one can study extinct cultures by means of this framework. This question cannot be answered completely by turning to philosophers of science, or by examining scientific procedures in other disciplines. Philosophers of science tell us, in clear, logical terms, what scientific methods are; and scientists of other disciplines provide various models demonstrating how these methods may be applied. But before scientific archeology can progress in an orderly and systematic fashion, archeologists must achieve preliminary general agreement concerning initial assumptions, proper procedures, and what constitute successful and acceptable general laws and explanations in archeology. This consensus must be worked out in practice by archeologists themselves, within the general scientific framework (see Harvey 1969 for an excellent example from a related discipline).

There has as yet been little progress along these lines. David L. Clarke has provided an impressive compendium of analytical procedures available to modern archeologists (Clarke 1968). These, of course, are necessary for scientific archeology but they do not suffice on their own, and we do not discuss them here because they are not prerequisite for the understanding of our presentation, which is predominantly a way of viewing archeological data, analysis, and interpretation. Similarly, we do not provide discussion and descriptions of excavation and other field techniques that are readily available elsewhere (Hole and Heizer 1969; Heizer and Graham 1967; Wheeler 1954). These must be used within a particular archeological and scientific framework that has yet to be agreed upon, and it is this framework that we are concerned with in this book.

Robert McC. Adams (1968) and Bruce G. Trigger (1968, 1970), although they utilize rather different approaches, both consider the history and present state of archeological method and address themselves to the question of whether anthropologically oriented archeology should indeed be explicitly scientific. Neither gives a simple answer to this question. Adams thinks archeology can certainly benefit from an explicitly scientific framework, but that this framework may not be the whole answer for archeologists. Trigger does not think archeology need be or should be explicitly scientific, but rather emphasizes its historical (narrative or descriptive) aspects (see Chapter 6, pp. 165–72).

However, there are archeologists who, like us, favor an overtly scientific orientation, and it is our purpose here to provide a coherent, comprehensive description of what science in archeology can and should mean. We support our position by pointing out its most significant actual and potential contributions to the study of prehistory and to the science of man. Our presentation is also meant in itself to be a contribution toward the goal of arriving at a scientifically based framework for archeology.

In Chapter 1 we outline the rudiments of the logic of science, stressing especially the fundamentals of explanation. This logical structure is basic to all that follows. In Chapter 2 we present examples that illustrate how some archeologists are attempting to work within an explicitly scientific framework as they seek explanations of their data. The important issue of consensus on goals and methods within anthropological archeology is given preliminary consideration.

Chapters 3 and 4 contain discussions of the concept of culture, and of how it can most profitably be utilized by archeologists. Considerable emphasis is placed on a definition of culture that focuses on empirically observable behavior rather than on shared ideas and norms. Two important explanatory frameworks are discussed in some detail: systems theory and the ecological approach.

In Chapters 5 and 6 we consider some important aspects of archeological method to demonstrate how the archeologist's assumption of the scientific approach structures and defines field operations and subsequent analyses. Attention is given first to the nature of the archeological record and its limitations, then to spatial distributions at archeological sites, to classification and typology, and finally to basic statistical techniques. In the closing section we examine in detail the topic of agreement or consensus among archeologists about the objectives of their discipline and the most appropriate ways to attain them.

Chapter 6 includes consideration of three topics: (1) the most effective means of organizing archeological field work concerned with problems of culture process; (2) the publication of archeological reports; (3) archeology as a social science and the nature of archeological theory, with a discussion of the current controversy centering on the goals of archeology: Should they be predominantly to develop and confirm general laws and theories, or to describe and explain particular cases? This discussion leads to a final consideration of the sought-after consensus or mutual agreement among archeologists on objectives and methods for their discipline. We believe such consensus must be based on the realization that the scientific framework is not only compatible with but is also essential to adequate historical description and explanation of particular events.

It must also be made clear what we are *not* doing in this book. We are not interested in showing where and how archeologists have not been scientific. Because few archeologists have claimed that their work is rigorously scientific, this would be a meaningless endeavor. Furthermore, we believe that in the present state of theoretical discussion, a model or synthesis of what scientific archeology must logically entail is very useful to students and may also be of considerable value to interested members of the profession as a means of crystallizing debate on the various issues.

The position we discuss here is not an invention of our own, or of a few other archeologists. It is in effect the general position of science. Its relevance to archeology is the result of a decision by archeologists to be scientific. We point out some of the most important logical consequences of this decision.

There are those who might consider the recent emphasis on scientific method in archeology to be little more than a rhetorical flourish, perhaps no more than a temporary terminological fad, while the actual work of archeologists does not change or become more scientific at all. We disagree with this view; the trend toward a scientific framework has deep roots in anthropological archeology. The recent emphasis on scientific rigor is neither a brand new development nor is it simply rhetorical; it is the result of a long-term trend that has now progressed far enough to attract the attention of the entire field.

We cannot stress too strongly, however, that we do not view this trend as necessarily leading toward a future in which all archeologists everywhere must be scientists. Many respected archeologists have carefully evaluated the scientific approach and are not interested in adopting it, because they feel that there are advantages to working outside an overtly scientific framework; this situation will doubtless continue.

There are, however, two things that must be made clear. First, although some archeologists reject a rigorously scientific archeology, it is here to stay, and we think it will come to dominate the field by providing standards against which all work will be evaluated. Second, there is an important place (as well as a need) for it within the social sciences, where prediction is as important as explanation. That is, archeologists can help to formulate and to test hypothetical laws of human and cultural behavior.

The distinction between archeologists who have a scientific orientation to archeology and those who do not has tended to produce some dissension among archeologists, though it should not. The polemical rhetoric of some archeologists on the topic of inherent differences between these two positions obscures the fact that in practice archeologists of both orientations work with and usefully employ the work of each other. This is important for scientific archeology because its practitioners use standard methods and techniques and must operate to a large extent with previously collected data, although the data may have been collected by persons with a different theoretical orientation and hence may be difficult to use.

Thus, those committed to the goals of scientific archeology must operate with a body of previously confirmed general laws, as well as with a body of pre-existing data. This is just a manifestation of the additive and self-corrective aspect of scientific methods and the search for explanations. Science proceeds by building upon already confirmed knowledge which does not need to be re-demonstrated at each succeeding step. But also, presently accepted explanations and laws can be refined and corrected only in the light of new scientifically obtained and confirmed conclusions. Hence, any scientist must demand from self-professed scientific colleagues equal dedication to the use of scientific methods, and recognition of the ramifications that acceptance of this position logically entails. A scientifically oriented archeologist should not demand that all archeologists must be overt scientists, but he does have the right to expect rigorous scientific procedure from those archeologists who claim to be contributing to an explicitly scientific archeology.

ACKNOWLEDGMENTS

WE SHOULD LIKE to acknowledge with gratitude the help given us by a number of different people. We are indebted to Richard A. Watson, who made detailed criticisms and comments on the successive drafts of the manuscript, who discussed the logic of science with us on numerous occasions, and who was an unfailing source of aid, advice, and encouragement throughout the entire affair. We are grateful to Linda Redman for cheerful and unflagging assistance in many ways, especially with much of the initial typing.

Various early versions of the manuscript were read and commented on by Robert McC. Adams, Lewis R. Binford, Dan Bowman, Robert J. Braidwood, David L. Browman, Kent V. Flannery, Maxine Haldemann-Kleindienst, James N. Hill, Frank Hole, Mark P. Leone, Albert C. Spaulding, Stuart Struever, and David Webster. We are very grateful to all of them, although they are not, of course, responsible for the manner in which we have interpreted their comments.

We should like to thank the Aldine Publishing Company for permission to use citations and tables from James Hill's paper ("Broken K Pueblo: Problems of Form and Function") published in *New Perspectives in Archeology,* Sally R. Binford and Lewis R. Binford, editors.

The original suggestion that we write this book came from Steven LeBlanc at the close of a seminar in archeological theory and method given by Patty Jo Watson at Washington University in 1969. The general orientation and much of the subject matter chosen for the seminar were a direct result of innumerable and interminable discussions, debates, and disputes between Patty Jo Watson and Charles Redman beginning in Turkey in 1968 and continuing at the University of Chicago's Oriental Institute and in Salts Cave, Kentucky, through the succeeding year. In the course of the Washington University seminar, we felt strongly the need for a book which would clearly set forth the framework of "new archeology" with emphasis on the logic of science, which we believe to be the heart of the matter. That is what we have attempted to do here.

We should like to close this prefatory note by acknowledging our immense debt to the writings of those archeologists—and other anthropologists such as Leslie White—who have been concerned with some of the same problems and questions we discuss in this book. We do not believe there is an unbridgeable gulf between the old archeology and the new, nor do we believe the new is a short-lived fad. Rather we agree with Bruce G. Trigger (1970) and Paul S. Martin (1971) that it is a development deeply rooted in anthropologically oriented archeology. The desire to contribute to this development has caused us to write this book.

PJW
SAL
CLR

February, 1971

CONTENTS

Part One

The Nature of Explanation
in Archeology

CHAPTER ONE

罒罒

THE LOGIC OF SCIENCE

ONE DISTINCTIVE FEATURE of scientific archeology is a self-conscious concern with the formulation and testing of hypothetical general laws.[1] General laws in archeology that concern cultural processes can be used to describe, explain, and predict cultural differences and similarities represented in the archeological record, and thus to further the ultimate goal of anthropology, which is the description, explanation, and prediction of cultural differences and similarities primarily in the present (L. Binford 1962, 1967b, 1968a, 1968b; Struever 1968b: 285–88; Fritz and Plog 1970). Emphasis on formulation and testing of general laws means that archeology is conceived as a formal scientific discipline with the same logical structure as all other scientific disciplines. In this chapter we discuss briefly the most pertinent aspects of the logic of science, and in the following chapter show how these topics are actually handled in selected examples from the literature of scientific archeology.

The crucial issues are *epistemological;* that is, they have to do with how we know, and how we know we know. These questions are the traditional concern of philosophers of science, one of

[1] By "general law," we mean the same as the "lawlike generalization" of Hempel and Oppenheim (1948, reprinted widely, e.g., in Feigl and Brodbeck 1953). See also Hempel 1965, and below, pp. 4ff.

the best known and most respected of whom is Carl G. Hempel. Hempel's writings on the logic of science are frequently referred to by scientifically oriented archeologists and are the primary source for the discussion presented here. The crucial epistemological issues can be summarized under three headings:

1. *Knowledge of the world.* The basic assumption of all science is that there is a real, knowable world. The empirically observable behavior of the entities which make up this real world is orderly and can be predicted and explained when adequate observation, hypothesis formulation, and hypothesis testing leading to the confirmation of general laws have been accomplished. Any empirically observable series of phenomena in the real world can be so investigated, logically speaking, though there may be practical or operational difficulties in doing so (Hempel 1966: 3 and Chapter 6 here). Stated in another way this means that science is deterministic and that scientists assume that general laws can be confirmed that will allow the explanation and prediction of the behavior of all empirically observable phenomena.

2. *Truth.* Although scientists must and do assume that there is a real, orderly, knowable world, they do not believe and cannot prove that any lawlike generalization is necessarily the final truth about reality. Scientists do not seek absolute certainty but must, again logically speaking, base their explanations on those hypotheses that are currently confirmed most adequately by appropriate tests. Just what constitutes "confirmation" and "appropriate testing" must be mutually agreed upon within each particular scientific discipline, and this extremely important issue is the focal point of considerable discussion, which we will not go into further here (but see pp. 11, 46–49 below). Clearly, however, this feature of the "modifiability" of laws in the light of new data or new tests means that the laws (and all explanations based on them) are simply statements most probably descriptive of regularities in the real world.

3. *Explanation and general laws.* Explanation in the logic of

science means "Subsumption of a phenomenon under a general law directly connecting observable characteristics . . ." (Hempel and Oppenheim in Feigel and Brodbeck 1953: 332). A scientist explains a particular event by subsuming its description under the appropriate confirmed general law, that is, by finding a general law that covers the particular event by describing the general circumstances, objects, and behavior of which the particular case is an example.

An explanation is not considered adequate unless the general laws and the statements describing the circumstances pertaining in the particular case in question logically could have enabled the observer to *predict* the particular case. This is sometimes referred to as the parity of explanation and prediction, which means that statements of explanation are logically equivalent to statements of prediction in any given case.

It is of some interest to note that the logical structure of a scientific *explanation* is identical with that of a scientific *prediction,* the only difference between them being the purely pragmatic one of the temporal vantage point of the inquirer. . . . *we have an explanation for an event if, and only if* (from a different temporal vantage point), *we could have predicted it* (Rudner 1966: 60).

A particular event is predicted before it occurs by referring to the general law of which this particular event and its circumstances are an instance, just as the particular event is explained after it has occurred by referring to the general law of which this event and its circumstances are an instance. The difference between explanation and prediction is not logical, but it is practical. It arises empirically because we can know and understand things and events only in a temporal context. Although there is an equivalence of logical structure between explanation and prediction, practically speaking, we can predict an event only if we know the general law and the circumstances for the particular event before the occurrence of that event. If the event has already occurred, we can explain it only by reference to the general law and the particular circumstances. We can also in this way "postdict" the occurrence of past events, and then look for evidence in the archeological record to test such "predictions about the past." A most important result of the logical equivalence is the fact that confirmed explanations are just what allow us to make reliable predictions about the future.

It is this potential predictive force which gives scientific explanation its importance: only to the extent that we are able to explain empirical facts can we attain the major objective of scientific research, namely not merely to record the phenomena of our experience, but to learn from them, by basing upon them theoretical generalizations which enable us to anticipate new occurrences. . . . (Hempel and Oppenheim in Feigl and Brodbeck 1953: 323)

It is a major goal of archeology to explain the past, but as indicated by Hempel and Oppenheim, all scientific explanations, including those in archeology, help to explain contemporary events and to predict future events.

The kind of explanation we are discussing is called deductive-nomological or deterministic or causal. "Deductive" means working from the general to the particular; in this case the explanation is deductive because the general law (also called the covering law) is given, and one explains the particular by subsuming it under this general law. "Nomological" refers to the science of general laws.

The general law to which the specific event is referred has a logical form which can be summarized briefly as: "In C, if A, then B." This means that for all A, in circumstances of type C, when an event of kind A occurs, an event of kind B also occurs or will occur. A statement of this form asserts that general connections or relations exist between specified events and can be called a causal or deterministic law only if it has been tested and adequately confirmed. Just what constitutes adequate confirmation is one of the most difficult problems in the philosophy of science. Obviously, that B always follows A in a given type of event is not always enough to lead us to assert that "In C, if A, then B" is in this instance a confirmed law. What is needed further for confirmation is difficult to characterize in general terms, but in practice one can usually find reasons for concluding that some "In C, if A, then B" assertions express deterministic or causal connections, while others reflect only contingent or accidental relations.

Statistical or "probabilistic" laws are especially characteristic of the social sciences and these, too, are deterministic. Nonstatistical laws determine particulars; statistical laws determine *groups* of particulars.

. . . generalizations in social science are usually probabilistic in character. Such generalizations claim only what is compatible with the observation of individual exceptions. Indeed, such assertions refer to no individual cases, but only to classes or sets of individual cases (Rudner 1966: 67).

An analogy drawn from the physical sciences helps clarify this point. A nuclear physicist can predict with great accuracy the half life, or rate of disintegration, of a radioactive element, even though he does not determine precisely when any individual atom of that element will decay. Similarly, a social scientist utilizing statistical or probabilistic laws about cultural processes can predict the results of such processes, even though he does not determine precisely the seemingly random events or decisions on the individual level.

In attempting to understand observed phenomena, the scientific investigator formulates trial explanations that are called hypotheses.[2] Such hypotheses make reference to hypothetical and/or confirmed laws that in the given circumstances appear to cover the particular events. Logically speaking, hypothetical laws —like hypothetical explanations—may be derived from any source whatever, although practically speaking they are usually

[2] The word "hypothesis" may be used more generally to mean any unconfirmed but testable proposition (Hempel 1966: 19).

suggested by observations made on the available data in combination with the observer's knowledge of related confirmed laws, and on his general background and experience. In the testing of either laws or of explanations (or of predictions), the crux of scientific procedure is that hypotheses are formulated tentatively and then tested empirically by a deductive procedure. From the general hypothesis one deduces statements describing particular things or events. Then one checks to see if these deduced statements do actually describe what is the case in the given circumstances. If they do, the hypothesis is so far confirmed.

This process can be described for hypothetical laws as follows: The hypothesis states a plausible relationship between two events under certain specific circumstances. The statement takes the form: "If an event of one kind occurs, an event of another kind will also occur."

To test this hypothesis, the investigator deduces from it propositions called test implications that must be exemplified in the world if the hypothesis is empirically correct. Ordinarily the investigator deduces several such test implications. Because the test implications follow from the hypothesis logically, they must be true of the world if the hypothesis itself is true of the world. However, the reverse is *not* necessarily the case: Because the test implication is found to be true of the world does not mean that the hypothesis must be. It simply means that the hypothesis may be empirically true because it has not been shown to be false (disconfirmed). That is, the general form of the law does not say that the test implication is true if and only if the hypothesis is true; it leaves open the possibility that the test implication could be true even if the hypothesis is false. For example, one might predict that if an ancient city had been set fire by invaders, one would find burned walls when he excavates the city mound. But finding the walls so burned does not necessarily confirm the hypothesis, because the burning might have been the result of an accidental fire.

The above discussion can be expressed in symbols as follows:

Let H (the hypothesis) = the relationship, "in C, if A, then B".
Let I = the test implication deduced from H.
Then if H is true, I is true.
I is found to be true.
H may or may not be true, but has not been disconfirmed.

So far we have considered the case where the test implication is found to be true. We now need to consider the consequences if the test implication is found to be false. Because the test implication has been deduced from the hypothesis and must be true of the world if the hypothesis is empirically true, the hypothesis must be false if the test implication is found to be false.

These relationships can be summarized as follows:

If H, then I.
Not I (that is, I is found to be false of the world).
Therefore, not H (that is, H must also be false).

Up to this point we have been discussing some basic rudiments of deductive logic. Now we turn to a consideration of inductive logic. Although in actuality the two processes are inseparable, a distinction is often made between inferences arrived at deductively and those arrived at inductively.

Inductive inferences are often described as leading from observations of particular cases to a conclusion that has the logical form of a general law or principle. "In X cases observed, whenever A occurs, then B occurs; therefore in similar circumstances, if A occurs, B will also occur." Even if the observations are true, the conclusion follows logically only for the domain of A's and B's actually observed. It does not follow logically for all possible A's and B's, because the very next observation and all succeeding ones for y number of cases may show no positive correlation between events of kind A and events of kind B. For this reason inductive generalizations, that is, hypotheses inductively generated, give us certainty only about those cases of which we are already sure.

However, inductive generalizations can be tested and confirmed (again a very difficult problem in the philosophy of science) with the result that the premises of an inductive inference can be taken to imply generalizations that have a more or less high probability of being true of the world. Deductive inferences differ from inductive ones by implying conclusions with logical necessity, but because the confirmation of the generalizations used in deductive inference depends on inductive techniques, they also are only probably true. That is, a conclusion may follow logically from a hypothesis by deductive inference, and then this conclusion may be found to be true of the world. The hypothesis is then so far confirmed. But there is no necessary completion of the testing of deductive implications because new test implications can be derived from the hypothesis or old test implications can be retested. Further, any discovery of an instance where what is implied by the hypothesis is found to be false of the world so far disconfirms the hypothesis.

It is widely believed that in scientific investigation it is simply inductive inference from previously collected data that leads to general principles which are then not thought to require further testing. This is the view that one first collects all the facts, analyzes them, classifies them, draws inductive generalizations from them, and then presents them as laws. This procedure has been called *"the narrow inductivist conception of scientific inquiry"* and is regarded as untenable by logical positivists (Hempel 1966: 11). "Narrow inductivist" means an approach which does not provide for the testing of the generalizations derived from observation of particulars. If untested, such generalizations are, strictly speaking, only unconfirmed hypotheses. When utilizing a deductive approach, one begins with the hypotheses (which might very well, but not necessarily, have been derived inductively) and explicitly tests them, as described above (pp. 6 ff.). *Hypotheses are necessary to give direction to research, to determine what further data should be collected, and to guide the analysis of the data.* One is unlikely to collect relevant data without knowledge of the hypotheses to which the data are to have relevance, and it is to this extent that assumed or confirmed generalizations necessarily guide the direction of research.

In the logic of science there are no general rules of induction for deriving generalizations from observation of particulars, or any for mechanically generating hypotheses or theories from empirical data alone. "The transition from data to theory requires creative imagination," but:

scientific objectivity is safeguarded by the principle that while hypotheses and theories may be freely invented and *proposed* in science, they can be *accepted* into the body of scientific knowledge only if they pass critical scrutiny, which includes in particular the checking of suitable test implications by careful observation or experiment (Hempel 1966: 15, 16).

We indicate above that in testing for the empirical truth of the implication of a deduction, one does not confirm the hypothesis by establishing the truth of the implications. In the absence of negative results, however, the degree of confirmation of the hypothesis is regarded as increasing with the number of favorable test findings and is especially strengthened by favorable results from a wide variety of tests. Diversity of evidence is an important factor in confirmation, as is new evidence (facts consistent with the hypothesis but not known or taken into account when it was formulated), simplicity of logical form (if each of two or more hypotheses account for the same data and do not differ in other respects relevant to their confirmation, the simplest one is usually taken to be the more acceptable), and consistency with other scientific knowledge at the time in question.

Likewise, in inductive inference from repeated observations to generalized conclusions, the addition of observations of particular examples of the paired events in the generalized conclusion (in C, if A, then B) with no negative instances increases the probability of the conclusion (although no number of positive instances can ever "prove" the conclusion). Working scientists, of course, often build hypotheses inductively on the basis of inference from observations, and then test these hypotheses by checking implications deduced from them. In fact, though some scientists may be more interested in inferring general conclusions than either in testing them or in using them to give explanations and to make predictions, the notions that there are empirical sciences that are solely either inductive or deductive, and that there are scientists who proceed solely either inductively or deductively, are totally misleading. The logic of empirical science in its completeness is a combination of inductive and deductive forms and procedures.

What has just been said about science is true of archeology conceived as a science. A common misconception about explicitly scientific archeology is that a definite excavation program of problems to be solved and hypotheses to be tested constitutes a framework so restrictive that the practicing archeologist alters neither his goals nor his procedures in the course of actual excavation. It is unscientific to excavate with no plan nor problem in mind to which the data might contribute a solution, but if one knew exactly what was in the ground before excavation, there would be no reason to dig. We know enough to pose hypotheses for which digging can in principle provide a test, but are not surprised if the excavation does not provide data for the precise testing of just those hypotheses with which we began.

Practically speaking, an archeologist who has committed a considerable amount of time and money in preparation, who has obtained permissions and transported personnel, and who has begun digging at a given site, cannot pull up stakes because the data being turned out of the ground appears to be less significant for his original hypothetical framework than he had hoped. What is demanded by explicitly scientific archeological procedure is that the archeologist take into consideration whatever data results from his excavation, altering his hypotheses if necessary and adjusting his tests in the light of this data. In extreme cases, as a result of particular combinations of circumstances, he may even have to abandon hypotheses, or—rarely—even his entire original plan in order to do justice to the material at hand. This might be unfortunate given his desire to solve certain kinds of problems, but it is not necessarily unscientific. Procedure by the method of hypotheses in science always involves modifying them as data accumulates, and sometimes rejecting them and substituting entirely different hypotheses.

Because it is impossible to collect all the data (Chapter 5) archeologists must constantly decide whether the information they are collecting justifies the necessary destruction of materials from which other information could be extracted. This is often a matter of personal interest and orientation; different archeologists excavating the same site would make different choices. It would be unrealistic, therefore, to suggest that an archeologist should ignore everything in his excavation except what bears directly on the hypotheses he wishes to test. For example, he may begin his excavations having planned for and anticipated recovering detailed data on subsistence at the chosen site. As work progresses he may find that the site also contains a series of subfloor burials accompanied by grave goods which apparently reflect status or rank. He must then decide whether to shift the focus of his study to make the most of this newly disclosed data, or whether to ignore them, or to come to some compromise objective. Situations of this sort arise frequently but there is less and less excuse today for the archeologist to be surprised by major blocks of totally unanticipated data (such as an unsuspected Roman occupation horizon obscuring a part of the Early Bronze Age community the archeologist wishes to investigate) that necessitate drastic modification of his hypotheses and plan of attack. If the archeologist has studied the available data as thoroughly as he should, if he has examined his site as carefully as he should in its environmental circumstances and with systematic surface surveys and test excavations, and if he has thought deeply and cogently about the problems he wishes to solve and the hypotheses he wishes to test, then as archeology continues to advance, major surprises will be more the exception than the rule. Although the archeologist is bound neither to the exact form of his original hypotheses nor even to the original set of hypotheses, he *is* bound to be explicit about what problems he hopes to solve and what hypotheses he means to test. Seldom will he excavate a site for which he has set out hypotheses that do not need modification in the light of the data. What he can anticipate with this procedure, however, is an increase of systematic knowledge.

That the conceptual understanding and expression of an archeologist's work develops in actual practice through interaction of a priori plan and hard data is well known. This is the ongoing dialogue between the scientist and his material. This procedure is not only legitimate but also it is the life of science. It means that a hypothesis that was suggested by excavation data and thus was formulated after the excavation was begun is legitimate. It is the case in archeology as in many other sciences that the data are seen to constitute tests of hypotheses or answers to problems that are as yet not explicitly formulated. It is the goal of scientific archeology to anticipate problems and hypotheses prior to accumulating the data pertinent to them, but obviously most problems and hypotheses are suggested by our comprehension of data similar to that we expect to find. The excitement of discovery that leads to innovation in science, however, stems directly from the fact that we do not know everything about our material.

Misunderstanding about how problems and hypotheses are formulated and modified in the light of data has led to a misguided criticism of explicitly scientific archeology. That is, some take it to be a criticism to say that explicit hypotheses have been formulated by some professedly scientific archeologists only *after* they have seen the data. It is thought to be unfair or illegitimate to generate the hypothesis from the data.

In logical terms, however, the order of genesis of problems, hypotheses, and the data pertinent to them is immaterial. For clear exposition of results, problems, hypotheses, and pertinent data are set out clearly to show their logical relations. This often gives the impression that the scientific work that got these results also proceeded in a straightforward, unproblematic way. But of course scientific work does not typically proceed as neatly as does a scientific report; it is the misconception that it does, or the even greater misconception that it should, that gives rise to the criticism that post hoc problems and hypotheses and their solutions and tests with pregathered data are not legitimate. Logically, which actually comes first is immaterial, because, logically, problems, hypotheses, solutions, and tests are atemporal; what is important is not the temporal order of their generation or presentation but their conceptual relations.

It must be stressed that in any circumstances the form of the deductive method is preserved in the demand that one's work must constitute a test of the hypotheses. In whatever way the hypotheses are generated, one's data must stand in a logical relation of being the test circumstances of the hypotheses, contributing to their confirmation or disconfirmation. Otherwise, the work is disjointed and does not exemplify the explicitly scientific approach.

Thus while there is good epistemological reason for ordering reports with problems and hypotheses clearly stated before supporting data is given, it is misleading to imply that this is or should invariably be the sequence by which scientific research proceeds, because this may suggest to potential critics and young scientists an ideal that is seldom exemplified in practice.[3]

The epistemological form of scientific knowledge—that is, the relations between hypotheses, data, and conclusions—suggests the general order of procedure for scientific investigations. Logically the order of procedure is not important, but practically there

---

[3] If any doubt remains about the distinction between conceptual knowledge and the infinite number of ways one can come to it, we recommend that the prospective critic of scientific archeology, as well as anyone interested in the way in which science is done, read James D. Watson's book *The Double Helix.*

is a world of difference between finishing an excavation and then defining one or more post hoc hypotheses, and defining a new hypothesis and its test implications while excavation is in progress. Completely post hoc hypotheses can be tested only by data that happens to be relevant to them. If, on the other hand, hypotheses are defined while work is still in progress, data relevant to the test implications can be deliberately collected, thus greatly increasing the likelihood that the hypotheses can be properly tested. While not discounting the scientific value of post hoc hypotheses, we believe that more systematic knowledge can be gained in archeology by beginning with a priori hypotheses to test. Therefore, although we are experienced in the practical difficulties of excavation, we insist on the necessary priority of theory. We claim that closely controlled, problem-oriented archeology can be done with present knowledge. And we believe that as archeologists realize the potential of the explicitly scientific approach, hard-science archeology will become the rule.

TESTING HYPOTHETICAL EXPLANATIONS

In the above exposition we have been concerned with the nature of hypotheses and hypothetical laws, and with the testing and confirmation of them. The logic of testing a hypothetical explanation is exactly the same as that for testing a hypothesis or hypothetical law. What is tested (and confirmed or not) in this case, however, is the explanation, not the law. That is, an explanation includes one or more general laws that are confirmed or accepted as given. To test the hypothetical explanation, one deduces test implications and checks them to see whether the particular case in question is covered by the included laws. The investigator is not checking or testing the laws themselves but only whether they explain the situation in question (that is, whether they account satisfactorily for the available data). If they do not, the laws are not said to be disconfirmed, but another general law or set of laws, that is, another explanation, must be sought. In this instance it is the *explanation,* not its included laws, that is disconfirmed. Even if the suggested explanation does not hold for the particular case in question, the included laws can remain confirmed or adequate in themselves. However, if the given laws suggest consequences that data persistently fail to exhibit, this provides occasion for changing one's focus to test the laws themselves, in the light of the data, for possible refinement or disconfirmation.

As stated above, explanations have the form of subsuming descriptions of particular cases under accepted or confirmed general laws. Often it is thought that mere consistency of a particular case with a general law is adequate to show that the case is an exemplification of the law, that is, that the law explains the case. However, this is logically the same as saying that a hypothesis is necessarily confirmed if the test implication is confirmed, and, as explained above (pp. 8–9), this is not correct. It is necessary, of course, that the case be consistent with the law, but this consistency alone is not sufficient to confirm the hypothetical explanation. This is because a given case can be consistent with several different hypothetical explanations. Thus some further implications must be deduced from both the law and its proposed particular instance. Then one checks these further implications (as described above) in order to test the explanation as a whole.

For example, suppose an archeologist working in the Southwestern United States finds, when analyzing the distribution of pottery over his site, definite clustering of particular design elements or pot types in particular geographic locations: Types A, B, and C are found preponderantly in the northern part of the residential area, while types D and E characterize the southern areas (see Longacre study, pp. 34–37). One possible explanation of this situation is that the people who made the pots were living in these separate areas because the way their society was structured was expressed in its residence patterns. Assuming female potters, we might explain this situation by saying the society was matrilocal, hence the women remained in the residential areas in which they were born, and that in this case there seemed to be two such matrilocal groups. Such a hypothetical explanation involves various basic assumptions or general laws:

1. Women are the potters in this society.
2. Pot designs—motifs and their placement—are handed down from mother or grandmother to daughter and granddaughter with innovation or copying from other than mother or grandmother being very rare.

etc.

If there are alternate explanations using other general laws or different combinations of general laws that also explain the data adequately, then a crucial test must be made to decide among possible explanations. For example, the pottery distribution might be explained by the existence of full-time potter-specialists or of pottery guilds living in two different parts of the site. One's task then is to deduce test implications that follow from this second explanation, but that cannot be true if the first explanation is the correct one. These implications might include the nature of the clusters themselves: If the pots were produced by guilds or master potters, the distinctive wares should be distributed differently within the village and within graves, and the distribution of pottery styles between villages would be different from those expected if matrilocality is the better explanation. A likely source of error in archeological interpretation, then, is not only inadequate testing of some one explanation but also failure to conceive of and to test alternate explanations.

While archeologists often talk of testing laws, most often they are testing explanations based on accepted laws, so the disconfirmation of the explanation should not necessarily lead them to reject the law as a law, but merely to reject it as the basis for an explanation of the case in hand. What they are searching for is the right law on which to base the explanation.

In the next chapter we provide some examples of the testing of hypothetical explanations and laws by archeologists.

CHAPTER TWO

THE LOGICAL STRUCTURE OF
AN EXPLICITLY SCIENTIFIC
ARCHEOLOGY

WE NOW TURN to the literature of scientific archeology. Because this approach, as a self-conscious posture, is new, the literature is not voluminous. One person, Lewis R. Binford, has been responsible for a large percentage of the theoretical writing on the subject; therefore the examples given below of necessity lean heavily on his publications and those of persons influenced by him. We do not, however, intend to summarize all the work of the archeologists to whom we refer but to utilize only that material which best illustrates the main points of our analysis:

1. *Knowledge of the world.*
2. *Truth.*
3. *Explanation and general laws.*

KNOWLEDGE OF THE WORLD

Binford summarizes the position of a scientific archeology with respect to knowledge of that aspect of reality—the past—which the archeologist wishes to investigate in order to formulate and test a variety of general laws and explanations:

We assume that the past is knowable; that with enough methodological ingenuity, propositions about the past are testable; and that there are valid scientific criteria for judging the probability of a statement about the past. . . . (L. Binford 1968a: 26).

Although much of the data archeologists work with derives from objects of "material culture," this does not mean the archeological record is lacking in all information concerning nonmaterial features of the extinct society. On the contrary, Binford insists that data relating to the entire extinct cultural system are present in the archeological record, a position pioneered by Taylor (1948: Chapters 5 and 6).

It is virtually impossible to imagine that any given cultural item functioned in a sociocultural system independent of the operation of "nonmaterial" variables (L. Binford 1968a: 21).

He goes on to say that in devising means to extract this information on nonmaterial variables we cannot restrict ourselves to knowledge of material culture. In order to explain observations made on the archeological record it is necessary to deal with "the full range of determinants which operate within any sociocultural system, extant or extinct. . . ." Thus the claim is that the limitations on our knowledge of the past lie in the inadequacy of our research designs and methods, not in the archeological record itself.

This is probably somewhat overstated. That is, even if all the material items of a culture are related to its nonmaterial aspects, the archeological remains may be so limited, altered, or destroyed that a complete description of the past cannot be reconstructed from them, not just because our techniques (or intelligence) are limited, but because the complete past simply is not reflected in the material that remains. The possibility of the material's being so limited that little knowledge can be gained from it is certainly real, but one cannot allow this possibility to prevent him from attempting to work out all aspects of past human behavior.

Hence, the theoretical position defined for a scientific archeology in Binford's statements is precisely that of all scientists as described in the first chapter. They assume that there is a real, knowable (empirically observable), orderly world; in this case, the real, knowable, orderly world is that of past human events and behavior patterns. Although the humans themselves are long dead, their patterned behavior can be investigated by the hypothetico-deductive method of science because archeological remains and their spatial interrelationships are empirically observable records of that patterning.

TRUTH

The scientific archeologist's position with respect to truth in his studies is that of all other scientists: He is not expecting to enjoy certainty, but regards as most probable those hypotheses which are most adequately confirmed at any one time.

The process theorists [1] assume that "truth" is just the best current hypothesis, and that *whatever* they believe now will ultimately be proved wrong, either within their lifetime or afterward. Their "theories" are not like children to them, and they suffer less trauma when the theories prove "wrong" (Flannery 1967).

Flannery here is referring to the scientist's attitude that the most adequately confirmed hypothesis available at the moment is simply the best available approximation to the truth.

Julian H. Steward made the same point some twenty years

[1] That is, archeologists who, like the proponents of new archeology, are interested in the general aspects of cultural processes rather than in the specific aspects of cultural history. "Cultural process" or "culture process" usually means the synchronic or diachronic functioning and interrelationships of the systems and sub-systems that comprise a particular culture or human society; that is, the way a culture works at any one point in time, or the way it changes through time. But the same terms are sometimes used to mean the general laws about such functioning.

ago in a well-known paper published in the *American Anthropologist,* "Cultural Causality and Law: A Trial Formulation of the Development of Early Civilizations":

. . . it is obvious that the minutiae of culture history will never be completely known and that there is no need to defer formulations until all archeologists have laid down their shovels and all ethnologists have put away their notebooks. Unless anthropology is to interest itself mainly in the unique, exotic, and non-recurrent particulars, it is necessary that formulations be attempted no matter how tentative they may be. It is formulations that will enable us to state new kinds of problems and to direct attention to new kinds of data which have been slighted in the past. Fact-collecting of itself is insufficient scientific procedure; facts exist only as they are related to theories, and theories are not destroyed by facts—they are replaced by new theories which better explain the facts. Therefore, criticisms of this paper which concern facts alone and which fail to offer better formulations are of no interest (Steward 1949: 24–25).

This recalls our earlier discussion (pp. 10–11 of Chapter 1) of the need for hypotheses (Steward's "trial formulations") to give direction to research.

EXPLANATION AND GENERAL LAWS

As stated in the first sentence of Chapter 1, a basic goal of scientific archeology is the same as that of anthropology: to establish general laws concerning cultural process (see footnote 1) that enable explanation of cultural differences and similarities.

Initially, it must be asked, "What are the aims of anthropology?" Most will agree that the integrated field is striving to *explicate* and *explain* the total range of physical and cultural similarities and differences characteristic of the entire spatial-temporal span of man's existence (L. Binford 1962: 217).

The aim of anthropological archeology is equated with this aim of anthropology:

Archeology shares with other anthropological sciences the aim of explaining differences and similarities among cultural systems. We are, therefore, concerned with cultural theory and processual arguments which treat problems of the interrelationship of cultural (and any other relevant class of) variables which have explanatory value. . . . advances in archeological theory are prerequisite to the achievement of broader anthropological goals. It is through theoretical advances and sound arguments of relevance that we can link our observations on the archeological record to particular questions on the operation of past cultural systems (S. Binford and L. Binford 1968: 2).

The Binfords are saying that there are two aspects of archeological theory. One consists of assumptions and propositions pertaining to the archeological record itself. These assumptions and propositions have to do with the origins of the materials included in the archeological record, and with the sources of variability in that record. By sources of variability is meant processes and circumstances that result in differences and similarities in the morphological, spatial, and temporal characteristics of artifacts, features and other architectural remains, and their interrelationships at an archeological site.

The other aspect of theory in archeology is the archeological record taken as a giant time-space laboratory for social science. The argument establishing the relevance of prehistory to social science runs as follows: Given that the subject matter of social science—human beings and their behavior—cannot ordinarily be subjected to experimental manipulation under controlled circumstances, then observations must be made and data collected in as many diverse situations as possible—including those made available to us by use of archeological methods and techniques—if we are to be able to formulate and to test general laws concerning this subject matter. The archeological record then can be viewed as one means by which human behavior can be investigated both diachronically and synchronically. Here the archeologist has an advantage over the ethnologist who is limited to synchronic or very short time-span observation of living peoples.

That is, the archeologist can examine the record of human behavior that took place over very long periods of time in many different parts of the world. Moreover, though the archeologist cannot dig up a language or the details of a kinship system, he has the advantage of direct access to immense quantities of behavioral data. The archeological record reveals in the static patterning of directly observable material what the people actually did in the past, not what they thought they did or what they said they thought they did. Thus, though the ethnologist may have the advantage of a greater quantity of comtemporary material to examine, the archeologist obviously has a more comprehensive picture for longer spans of time.

But archeology cannot provide this time-space laboratory unless archeological methods are adequately developed so that cultural events and processes of significance to general cultural theory can be recognized in the archeological record and analyzed by archeologists. Furthermore, advances in the development of general cultural explanations may shift attention to variables not previously considered important, but now regarded as crucial for the explanation of cultural differences and similarities.

In such a case the hope would be that archeological data could be used in testing hypotheses drawn from theories of general anthropological interest. The ability of archeologists to maximize advances in culture theory depends on the existence of a viable and progressive body of archeological theory and method (S. Binford and L. Binford 1968: 2–3).

Hence, much of the work of scientific archeologists (and therefore much of the content of this book) has been directed toward the development of archeological methods designed to elicit information concerning significant cultural events and processes from the archeological record (pp. 54–56). These methods and the resulting information are necessary prerequisites to the contributions archeology can make to anthropology and the whole of social science. In the last few pages of this chapter and in Chapter 6 we consider this larger topic of the relevance of archeology to the social scientist's quest for general laws that can be used to explain and to predict human behavior.

Fritz and Plog (1970) are very explicit with respect to the necessity for incorporating the logic of science in archeological research: "All archeologists employ laws in their research. Those of us who are interested in processual analysis have made the formulation and testing of laws our goal" (Fritz and Plog 1970: 405).

Their work, however, seems more oriented to formulating explanations that use laws that are themselves not explicitly tested. It is the explanation that is tested and confirmed or not. The laws in disconfirmed explanations are not necessarily rejected as laws, but only as the bases of explanation in the given case. It is true that laws are being tested to the extent that if one is found that is not useful in any given explanation, that law might be rejected (and thus disconfirmed as a law); but, ordinarily, accepted or confirmed laws are used to formulate hypothetical explanations for a given case. The laws themselves are usually neither formulated nor explicitly tested by the archeologist; his primary concern is almost always with the formulating and testing of explanations of given cases. However, archeologists are uniquely situated to formulate and to test evolutionary laws about human behavior (Chapter 6: 164).

As a specific example of some of the controversy surrounding the conception of explanation in archeology (which should be, as discussed in pp. 4–19 here, logically the same as explanation in any science), we refer to two articles published in the *Southwestern Journal of Anthropology* (Sabloff and Willey 1967, L. Binford 1968c). Sabloff and Willey state that it is necessary for archeologists to deal with processual questions, but that accurate historical reconstruction must be done first. To illustrate this they enumerate observations made on archeological data from the Lowland Maya area in the ninth century A.D. and suggest that an adequate explanation of the available data must include postulation of an invasion of the southern lowlands.

One would disagree with their insistence on giving first priority to historical reconstruction *if* what they seek is explanation. The crux of the disagreement lies in what is meant by "explanation." As we use the term, an explanation is a confirmed statement that subsumes a given case under an accepted law. Any historical reconstruction is replete with such subsumptions, whether these explanations are implicitly or explicitly expressed. What a scientific archeologist would object to is the assumption that the explanations that occur in the reconstruction are correct without test, or that they are untestable, or that they are inviolable, or even that they are not explanations but just some sort of "plain story." *All* stories contain explanations which must be subjected to test, and so must the laws underlying them also be subjected to test if they have not previously been confirmed.

For example, a documented invasion occurring prior to regional collapse might be grounds for a satisfactory explanation to historians who are interested in the particular sequence of events and who are willing to rely on widely accepted assumptions about cultural processes, such as the implicit law that regional collapse follows invasion. But it should be clear that: (1) This reliance on untested implicit assumptions is disallowed by the methodology of science and should not be condoned by scientific archeologists, who insist on formulating assumptions explicitly in hypothetical explanations to test them in order to confirm or disconfirm them. (2) Ideally, the scientist's goal is *confirmed* explanations that subsume particular events (for instance, the collapse of the Lowland Maya) under the appropriate, separately confirmed general law or laws. In some cases he may even formulate and test hypothetical laws, but usually—again—explanations are his main concern, and *unconfirmed* explanations are what he objects to.

What is the appropriate general law under which we can subsume (and thus explain) the collapse of the Lowland Maya? At the present time no such general law has been confirmed, but if we were to make explicit (formulate as hypotheses) the implicitly assumed laws of culture process included in references to invasions as explanations, and then test these hypothetical laws, we could, logically speaking, arrive at confirmed general laws of culture process which might explain the Maya case.

Assumptions implicit in references to invasions as explanations would include the following: An invasion occurs when someone for some reason wants to invade; it occurs when a society for some reason is in a vulnerable or weakened condition. If the society cannot resist pressures of hostile aliens and an invasion occurs, there may result decimation of the native population, disruption of the economy and communication systems, widespread destruction of property, forcible removal of the native power structure and substitution of a new power structure administered by the alien invaders, and so on.

Sometimes historical reconstructions utilizing "historical explanations" (that is, the detailing of particularistic sequences of events which are made intelligible by reference to implicit, plausible, but untested general laws about human behavior and culture process) are assessed only by evaluating the competence (experience, honesty, and scholarly ability) of the person proposing the reconstruction. More explicit tests are often not made because most interested historical scholars accept the implicit, untested behavioral and processual laws as grounds for a perfectly adequate explanation *if* the proposed sequence of events actually occurred. The main question to them is not whether the laws are confirmed (they implicitly assume that they are or could be), but whether the historian proposing the explanation is a good scholar who has the facts to support his explanation (that is, has adequate control of all the relevant historical evidence, has interpreted it carefully, and therefore has been able to infer the sequence of events accurately).

Binford, however, insists that if we are to be anthropologists and social scientists rather than nonscientifically oriented historians, it is our business to formulate these implicit assumptions as explicit hypothetical laws and explanations and then to test them.

If and when the hypothetical laws are confirmed, they can be used to provide hypothetical explanations of particular cases or events, which explanations in turn are tested. Obviously such laws and explanations are closely related, and may be formulated and tested concurrently. That is, given data may suggest an explanation that depends on an unconfirmed law. The law is formulated and then tested by checking to see whether it does in fact explain this and other similar but independent data. At the same time, the explanation is being tested. This procedure is not circular, for even though some of the same data may be used to formulate and to test both the law and the explanation, their separate confirmations (or disconfirmations) are logically distinct and depend on further independent and relevant data.

Explanation begins for the archeologist when observations made on the archeological record are linked through laws of cultural or behavioral functioning to past conditions or events. Successful explanation and the understanding of process are synonymous, and both proceed dialectically—by the formulation of hypotheses (potential laws on the relationships between two or more variables) and the testing of their validity against empirical data. Hypotheses about cause and effect must be explicitly formulated and then tested (L. Binford 1968c: 270).

In this passage Binford is stating what Sabloff and Willey should have been doing if they wished to operate explicitly as social scientifically oriented archeologists rather than as historically oriented archeologists. The implicit structure of their procedure is scientific in the sense accepted here. But the laws and explanations, and their justifications, must be made explicit for critical scientific communication to take place. A considerable number of old archeological reports could, in fact, be made "new" by rewriting that draws out the implicit assumptions. One must be wary of rejecting as unscientific work in which laws and explanations are merely implicit but are obvious and testable or even tested, nonetheless. Most "new" and many "old" archeologists have the same goals in mind: laws and explanations of human behavior in the past. Much of the refinement of the new archeology is contained in the explicit awareness of the need to test, and in the explicit exposition of laws and explanations in their descriptions of what men did in the ancient past. It is our task to formulate hypotheses that enable us to relate archeological remains to the events or conditions in the past which produced them, so that we can give explanations of past human behavior. With reference to the ancient Maya example, this means we must seek to establish criteria for recognizing in the archeological record the remains of such processes as invasions. What does the record of an invasion (and the attendant circumstances that might be specified in a culture processual law) look like archeologically? To answer this question and thus to establish an archeological corollary to the general processual law, one would have to test other hypothetical general laws, for example, that temporal continuity in the formal properties of artifacts varies directly with social continuity. That is to say that where the archeological record shows an abrupt breaking-off in distribution of artifacts and architecture of one kind and their replacement by another kind, the social units responsible for the two sets of material were also discontinuous (that is, different). Considerable refinement of such laws, and explicit deductions of their implications for the archeological record, would be necessary before they could be tested.

When confirmed, such laws linking archeological remains to cultural processes and events enable archeologists to use general processual laws to explain situations like that of the Lowland Maya. Such use of the data of prehistory makes it available to social science as a whole.

Once laws about cultural processes and events that show what archeological remains are to be expected have been formulated and confirmed, the archeological record can be used in turn to formulate and test further hypothetical laws. This is true for two reasons. First, the archeological record affords many more examples of results of such processes and events than are available historically or ethnographically. Hence, the archeological record represents a potential source of large quantities of independent data for testing laws about those processes and events. Second, archeologists can:

. . . contribute independent data to theories of sequence of forms and rate of change of at least some aspects of customary behavior. The chronological data are clues to the identification of antecedent and consequent conditions in slow-moving cultural transformations (Spaulding 1968: 38).

Here Spaulding explicitly recognizes that the unique contribution of archeology as a science is in evolutionary anthropology (see p. 164 below).

Binford concludes that:

. . . there is a necessary first step in archaeological research—the attempt to explain observations made on the archaeological record by hypothesis formulation and testing. It has been stressed that this step *necessarily* involves coping with problems of process. We attempt to explain similarities and differences in archaeological remains in terms of the functioning of material items in a cultural system and the processual features of the operation or evolution of the cultural systems responsible for the varied artifact forms, associations, and distributions observable in the ground (L. Binford 1968c: 273).

Binford states in his comments (1968c: 269 ff.) that Sabloff and Willey are advocating an intuitive and inferential approach (what Hempel calls "the narrow inductivist approach," p. 10 above) when they state "the best way to get answers to the processual problems connected with the fall of the Maya is through the building of a proper historical framework," and that "by first gaining control of the historical variables we will then be in an excellent position to eventually gain control of the processual ones" (Sabloff and Willey 1967: 330).

What Binford means is that Sabloff and Willey are advocating the derivation of general principles from previously collected data alone and are making no provision for testing the general principles by deducing test implications from them and checking the implications against independent data. To the contrary, an explicitly scientific approach must emphasize the deductive methods previously discussed (pp. 8–12).

Whatever one thinks of the sometimes pretentious expression of this insistence on self-conscious use of scientific method, one lasting beneficial result will be that archeologists henceforth will be forced to make their assumptions explicit. Unconfirmed laws and explanations may still be appealed to, but it will no longer be possible for either the archeologist or his readers to fail to see the status of these laws and explanations. So when archeologists emphasize a positivistic, deductive approach—the scientific method or method of hypothesis—they are often asking for little more than that assumptions and reasoning be made explicit:

. . . the ideas and theories of science are old, . . . however, in the field of archaeology these ideas are revolutionary. Most of my own efforts and those of my colleagues in the "new archaeology" have been directed toward the disproof of the old principles of interpretation which gave the ring of plausibility to traditional reconstructions and interpretations. We seek to replace these inadequate propositions by laws that are validated in the context of the epistemology of science, so that we may gain an accurate knowledge of the past (L. Binford 1968c: 274).

And so when Binford goes on to say that his paper

. . . . is one more attempt to demonstrate that a change in methodology is needed so that archaeologists will begin to test the validity of explanatory principles currently in use and attempt to refine or replace them by verified hypotheses relating the significance of archaeological data to past conditions.

it is not so much a radical change in method that he is calling for, as a refinement of and emphasis on *scientific* method in archeology.

In summary, it should be clear that Sabloff and Willey's explanation of the collapse of the Lowland Maya by a postulated invasion is not itself unscientific. It is only unconfirmed. What Binford is saying is that the means by which the explanation was arrived at is unscientific because only by testing scientific explanations of phenomena (admittedly a difficult and often tedious affair) can we build and establish confirmed statements about those phenomena. With reference to archeology this is a double task: First, we must confirm (if not formulate) general laws relating the processes or events in question (such as the collapse of high civilizations) to the archeological remains in order to find out in what ways the collapse is archeologically recorded. Second, we must formulate explanations of individual cases, for example, to explain why the Mayan civilization collapsed. The second task involves subsumption of any particular case of collapse under the appropriate general law or laws. Sabloff and Willey suggest invasion as an important factor in the collapse of the Lowland Maya. We agree with Spaulding (1968) and the logical positivist philosophers of science that there is no scientific explanation other than that which refers to general or covering laws, as described in outline here, pp. 4–16 above. Therefore, if invasion is to explain the collapse of the Lowland Maya, then appeal must be made to a confirmed general law of cultural process, of which the Mayan example is a particular instance. However, no such culture processual law has yet been confirmed. Hence, in order to explain what happened to the Lowland Maya, priority must be given to testing such processual laws to be applied to such cases.

A few recent studies exemplifying the formulation and testing of hypothetical laws that relate archeological data to past processes and conditions have been carried out (Deetz 1965; Dethlefson and Deetz 1966; Longacre 1966, 1968; Hill 1966, 1968, 1970a; Whallon 1968). We use the work of Longacre and Hill to illustrate how archeologists may define problems, generate hypothetical explanations, test the hypotheses, and rate them as confirmed or not.

In the following sections we utilize data from the published accounts of Longacre and Hill, not because they have more scientific merit than others, but because they best illustrate the points we want to make. We are not attempting to summarize everything they did, but we are using only those portions of their work which are most relevant to our discussion.

CARTER RANCH PUEBLO

Longacre's study at Carter Ranch Pueblo began in the summer of 1959 and was carried out in eastern Arizona during the three succeeding summers. In 1963 he completed his doctoral dissertation utilizing the data from the field work (Longacre 1963, 1966, 1968).

The primary focus is on the Carter Ranch Pueblo (*ca.* A.D. 1050–1200), where we attempted to isolate and explain certain organizational features of the sociocultural system as an initial step toward gaining a better understanding of adaptive changes made by the society to environmental stress (Longacre 1968: 89).

The basic assumptions underlying the work are as follows (see discussions in Chapters 3 and 4 here)—Culture is:

a systemic whole composed of interrelated subsystems, such as the social system, the technological system, the religious system, etc. . . . Such a perspective compels the paleoanthropologist to focus on the nature and interrelations of the component parts of the cultural system under study, and to work within an ecological frame of reference. The aim is to isolate and define cultural processes, the means by which cultures remain stable or change (Longacre 1968: 91; Chapter 3 here).
. . . the patterning of material remains in an archeological site is the result of the patterned behavior of the members of an extinct society and . . . this patterning is potentially informative as to the way the society was organized. Our first task, then, is to define the structure of the archeological remains at a site and to offer hypotheses as to the organization of the society and associated patterns of individual behavior. The patterned relationships among classes of artifacts should document the context in which they were made, used, and lost or

abandoned. It is essential to measure the mutual covariation among all classes and types of archeological data; the structure of this covariation, once delimited, should reflect the organizational and behavioral aspects of the society that produced it (Longacre 1968: 91; Chapter 5 here).

In his work in the Carter Ranch area Longacre wanted to investigate relationships between the sociocultural system and the environment, specifically what changes occurred in the former under conditions of environmental stress. Before he can investigate these relationships, he must be able to describe not only the paleo-environment but also the sociocultural system before, during, and after the environmental stress. Hence he designs his research procedures to elicit social organization from potsherds, burials, stone and bone tools, and the other cultural debris of a prehistoric pueblo. He begins by following work of Deetz (1960, 1965) and Cronin (1962: 105 ff.) in utilizing a basic assumption derived from ethnographic data:

. . . if there were a residence rule which led to related females living in the same locale through several generations, then ceramic manufacture and decoration would be learned and passed down within the context of this residence unit (assuming female potters) (Longacre 1968: 97–98).

Treating this assumption as a law, he formulates a hypothetical explanation with the conclusion that there was such a residential pattern at Carter Ranch Pueblo: Related females lived in the same locale through several generations. His explanation consists of subsuming the Carter Ranch case under the general law noted above concerning certain behavior patterns of women living in the same locale generation after generation. But he does not know whether this is a valid explanation of the Carter Ranch case or not; the explanation is hypothetical and unconfirmed. To begin to confirm it he deduces test implications from the hypothetical explanation and checks them. His first test implication is the following: If there were such a residence pattern at Carter Ranch, then we would expect female skills such as ceramic manufacture and decoration to be passed down within the context of this residence unit, and hence nonrandom distribution of designs should occur in the archeological record.

To check the test implication, Longacre defines 175 design elements and element groups taken from more than 6000 sherds and some whole vessels. He tabulates the distribution of these designs (counts how many of each kind occurred in which rooms and on which floors) and by statistical analyses elicits those designs that are persistently associated. Two clusters result, one comprising a block of rooms at the south end of the pueblo, the other comprising a room block at the north end of the pueblo. Thus the archeological record provides confirming evidence for the hypothetical explanation.

Longacre also derives several other implications, each to be checked against independent data. The most interesting among them is the following: If there were such a residence pattern, then the pottery with burials of the separate residence units should show nonrandom distribution of designs correlating with the distribution within each of the residence units.

To use this implication to test his hypothesis, he analyzes thirty-four burials excavated at the site. The burials occur in three clusters—north, south, and central—with each cluster having a different orientation pattern (east-west in the northern cluster, north-south in the southern cluster, and mixed in the central cluster). The northern burial area has pottery with designs like those in the northern room cluster and the southern group has pottery with designs like those in the southern room cluster; the center is mixed. The central burial cluster also shows many more ceremonial items included as grave offerings, and appears to represent burials of high status individuals from each of the separate residence units.

Thus the implications are found to be represented in the archeological record; hence the hypothetical explanation is so far confirmed. In the absence of valid alternate explanations (p. 18), the Carter Ranch case can be subsumed under the general law concerning certain behavior patterns of women living in the same locale generation after generation.

BROKEN K PUEBLO

Hill's field work was carried out in the summers of 1962–1963 at Broken K Pueblo very near the Carter Ranch site (both sites are in the Hay Hollow Valley just east of Snowflake, Arizona).

Hill's objectives are:

(1) to describe the locational patterning of various kinds of cultural features at the site, (2) to offer explanations of the demonstrated patterning in terms of past behavior, and (3) to test the accuracy of these explanatory propositions. This is intended as a case study in the demonstration of 'activity-areas' or 'activity-structure' within prehistoric communities. . . . I have attempted to illustrate a means by which it is possible to go beyond merely making inferences about past behavior; we can also test these inferences, and gain confidence (or lose confidence) in their validity. This can be done, even in those cases in which direct ethnographic evidence is not available (Hill 1968: 104).

On a more specific level, Hill is concerned with the variability in formal characteristics of the fifty-four pueblo rooms he excavated.

In order to explain the formal variability (in a behavioral or functional sense), it was first necessary to define the differences among the rooms in a clear and rigorous fashion (Hill 1968: 107).

Four of the excavated rooms are clearly different from all others. These special rooms "contained a number of peculiar features not common to the other rooms, including wall niches, benches, and a peculiarly designed firepit-ventilator combination."

Formal variability among the other rooms is more difficult to define. He selects several classes of attributes as measures of these differences:

1. Size (floor-area)
2. Firepits (presence or absence)
3. Mealing bins (presence or absence)
4. Ventilators (presence or absence)
5. Doorways (presence or absence)
6. Height of door sill
7. Masonry style

Data pertaining to these attribute classes are tabulated, and then manipulated statistically by use of the Chi-Squared test of association and the Fisher Exact Test (p. 141 below). These tests are used to demonstrate variability in distribution of room attributes and other categories of cultural remains. Factor analysis (pp. 148–49 here) is also employed to elicit nonrandom clusters of pottery types.

The results of the analysis are clear. . . . There were, in addition to the four special rooms, two other kinds of rooms—large rooms containing firepits, mealing bins, and ventilators, and small rooms that did not have such features.

The evidence thus far indicates that the variations in rooms at Broken K are analogous to the variations in rooms found in modern pueblos—large rooms with firepits and mealing bins . . . , small rooms lacking certain features, and special rooms containing a set of peculiar features of their own. . . . There is an additional analogue that would appear to clinch the case. In addition to the fact that the formal properties of the prehistoric and historic rooms are similar, the relative proportions of the room-types are similar (Hill 1968: 109, 115).

In contemporary pueblos large rooms analogous to those at Broken K are habitation or living rooms, the small rooms are storage rooms, and the special rooms are ceremonial rooms. Each household or segment of a lineage occupies a block of rooms including at least one habitation room and one or more storage rooms.

Given all of these analogies, it seems reasonable to state the proposition that the variability in rooms at the site has the same behavioral context as does the variability in modern pueblo rooms; the respective room-types are functional equivalents. It would not, however, be profitable to terminate the analysis at this point, as is so often done; the proposition must first be tested (Hill 1968: 116).

Hill then deduces a series of sixteen test implications utilizing his knowledge of activities in contemporary pueblos. His reasoning is as follows in terms of the logical framework established in the preceding part of this chapter (we refer to only a few of the sixteen implications as examples): On the basis of the general considerations described above, Hill infers that the rooms at the archeological site of Broken K Pueblo were functionally similar to those in contemporary pueblos. This inference can be stated in the form of a hypothetical general law, although the law is of limited scope because of the specificity of the circumstances: If the *formal* characteristics of Broken K Pueblo rooms are the same or closely similar to those in contemporary pueblos, the *functional* characteristics are also the same or closely similar. This law is important to Hill's work because, if confirmed, it will enable him to move from knowledge of material objects and their distributions to knowledge of prehistoric behavior (see pp. 54–56). Also, confirmation of the law will be *ipso facto* confirmation of a hypothetical explanation for various aspects of the Broken K archeological materials. Hence Hill's work can be viewed as a test of both a hypothetical general law and a hypothetical explanation accounting for certain aspects of his archeological data.

From the hypothetical law Hill deduces sixteen implications, utilizing his knowledge of activities in contemporary pueblos. Some examples follow.

I_1 If the large rooms were all-purpose living rooms, they ought to contain larger numbers and higher densities of most categories of cultural remains than either the small rooms or the special rooms. If the small rooms were storage rooms, they should have the lowest densities of most materials, with the exception of food crops; and the special rooms should fall somewhere in between.

I_2 The large rooms should contain a wider variety of materials than are found in the other room-types, since the largest number of different kinds of activities were presumably performed in them.

I_8 The small rooms, in addition to containing only a small number and variety of artifacts and manufacturing debris, should contain reasonably large quantities of the remains of stored food crops—especially corn and squash (since beans do not preserve well). This evidence should be in the form of corn cobs, seeds, or pollen.

I_9 The small rooms can be expected to contain evidence of some of the ethnographically recorded storage techniques, although most of the traces of these techniques would almost certainly not have been preserved. These rooms can, however, be expected to contain more large undecorated jars than do the other rooms, since the ethnographic evidence indicates that such jars are often used in storing various kinds of materials.

I_{12} The special rooms should contain evidence of ritual activities, independent of the peculiar structural features noted. They might, for example, contain the remains of idols, fetishes, or other presumably ceremonially related materials. They might also be expected to contain special types of pottery, and they should contain large quantities of seeds or pollen of the domestic crops, corn and squash. They may even yield a variety of wild plants that are used for ritual purposes in the present-day pueblo kivas.

I_{16} It can be expected that the three major kinds of rooms at the site did not all have the same context with regard to the sexual division of labor. The special rooms should contain cultural items associated with male activities primarily, while the large and small rooms should contain both male- and female-associated items (Hill 1968: 120–21).

CHECKING THE IMPLICATIONS
TO TEST THE HYPOTHETICAL LAW

I_1 and I_2. See Tables 2.1 and 2.2.

There can be no doubt that the first two propositions are confirmed; the large rooms contained not only the largest numbers and highest

TABLE 2.1.   DISTRIBUTION OF ARTIFACT TYPES

Artifact Type	Mean No. per Large Room	Mean No. per Small Room	Mean No. per Special Room	Total	Dominant Room-type	
Projectile Points	.92	.08	.50	27	L	P
Arrowshaft Tools	.88	.11	.00	25	L	
Antler Flakers	.08	.08	.25	5		P
Saws	.28	.04	.00	8	L	
Graver-Burins	.20	.20	.00	10	L S	
Flake Knives	1.70	.23	.00	48	L	
Bifacial Knives	.20	.07	.00	7	L	
Utilized Flakes	2.40	1.00	2.00	96	L S P	
Blades	.16	.16	.00	8	L S	
Cores	.92	.23	1.50 *	35	L	P
Scrapers	3.00	.84	3.00 *	108	L	P
Choppers	2.60	.44	4.70 *	96	L	P
Axes	.32	.00	.00	8	L	
Mauls	.28	.11	.00	10	L	
Hammerstones	3.70	.69	2.00 *	118	L	P
Metates	1.10	.15	.25	32	L	
Manos	6.60	1.00	.25	192	L	
Worked Slabs	.88	.15	.75	29	L	P
Worked Sherds	1.50	.15	.25	42	L	
Bone Awls	1.60	.27	.25	48	L	
Bone Rings and Ring Material	1.00	.11	.25	30	L	
"Ornamental" Items	.96	.19	.50	31	L	P

L = large room; S = small room; P = special room.
* All from a single special room (room beneath Room 41).
(Hill 1968: 122, Table 2).

densities of most cultural materials at the site, but also the widest variety of materials (Hill 1968: 122; see Table 2.1).

The large rooms also contain most of the lithic waste, animal bone, and plant remains (Table 2.2). Finally:

> the factor analysis of pottery types (which yielded non-random clusters of covarying types) revealed that there was a larger variety of different kinds of pottery in the large rooms than in either of the other two kinds of rooms (Hill 1968: 123; see Tables 2.3, 2.4).

TABLE 2.2.   DISTRIBUTION OF NON-ARTIFACT MATERIALS

Item	Mean No. per Large Room	Mean No. per Small Room	Mean No. per Special Room
Lithic Waste	98.0	30.0	37.0
Animal Bone	120.0	26.0	29.0
Seeds	9.3	4.2	2.5
Pollen Grains (economic)	22.0	51.0	17.0

(Hill 1968: 123, Table 3).

I_8 The small rooms also yielded a great deal of the expected evidence. In addition to having only small quantities of most materials, they yielded good evidence that they had been used for storing food crops . . . this evidence was largely palynological. The pollen of economic plants was much more abundant on the floors of the small rooms than on those of either of the other room types (see Table 2.2). Most of the pollen samples from small rooms contained more than 43 grains of economic pollen each, while the large rooms generally had between 0 and 42 grains. A Fisher Exact Test revealed that there is less than one chance in a thousand that this distribution is in error (.001 level). A separate test was performed using the frequencies of *Zea* and *Cucurbita* alone, with exactly the same results. The special rooms had surprisingly small quantities of economic pollen.

This great density of economic pollen in the small rooms clearly indicates that crops were being stored in these rooms (Hill 1968: 128–29).

I_9 The small rooms, instead of containing significant numbers of large textured storage jars, were characterized primarily by the presence of bowls (Hill 1968: 129).

Both the factor analysis and the raw frequencies of pottery types by room yield this same result.

The only pottery-type factor of importance in the small rooms was factor 6 (McDonald Plain Corrugated and St. Johns Polychrome), and the vessel forms are both bowls (Hill 1968: 129; see Table 2.3).

With respect to the sherd counts:

While large unpainted jars (sherds) did occur in the small rooms, their frequencies were much lower than in either the large or special rooms. . . . Thus while the palynological evidence supports the idea that the small rooms were storage rooms, the pottery-type evidence does not. (Hill 1968: 129–30)

I_{12}. The special rooms do not contain easily recognizable cult objects or ceremonial paraphernalia, but they do contain a peculiar combination of pottery types. The dominant pottery-type factors are, in order of importance:

Special Rooms	Factors
Room 6	7, 4
Room 29	1, 4
Room beneath Room 41	4, 3, 7
Room in N.W. corner of plaza	1, 3

(Hill 1968: 131)

TABLE 2.3.   POTTERY-TYPE FACTORS

Factor Number	Pottery Types	Vessel Forms
1	Patterned Corrugated	Jars
	Pinto Polychrome	Bowls
	Brown Indented Corrugated	Jars
2	Brown Plain Corrugated (Smudged Interior)	Bowls
	Tularosa Black-on-White	Jars, Bowls
3	Snowflake Black-on-White (Snowflake Variety)	Jars, Bowls
4	Brown Plain Corrugated	Jars
	Brown Indented Corrugated	Jars
5	Brown Indented Corrugated (Smudged Interior)	Bowls
	McDonald Indented Corrugated	Bowls
	Snowflake Black-on-White (Hay Hollow Variety)	Bowls, Jars
6	McDonald Plain Corrugated	Bowls
	St. Johns Polychrome	Bowls
7	St. Johns Black-on-Red	Bowls

Bowl and jar forms are given in order of frequency.
(Hill 1968: 124, Table 4).

TABLE 2.4. DISTRIBUTION OF POTTERY TYPES

(Room Categories in Which Pottery Types Are Dominant, as
Determined by Factor Analysis)

Pottery Type	Large	Small	Special
Brown Plain Corrugated (Smudged Interior) (B)	X		
Brown Indented Corrugated (Smudged Interior) (B)	X		
McDonald Indented Corrugated (B)	X		
Tularosa Black-on-White (J, B)	X		
Snowflake Black-on-White (Hay Hollow Variety) (B, J)	X		
Brown Indented Corrugated (J)	X		X
Patterned Corrugated (J)	X		X
Snowflake Black-on-White (Snowflake Variety) (J, B)	X		X
Pinto Polychrome (B)	X		X
Brown Plain Corrugated (J)			X
St. Johns Black-on-Red (B)			X
McDonald Corrugated (B)		X	
St. Johns Polychrome (B)		X	

B = bowl; J = jar.
(Hill 1968: 127, Table 5).

Factors 1, 3, 4, and 7 are commonly found in the special
rooms and represent the major pottery types used in those rooms
(see Tables 2.3, 2.4). Factors 2 and 5, which are strongly represented in the large rooms, are not important in the special rooms;
nor is factor 6 (the small-room factor). Basing himself on some of
Longacre's findings, Hill suggests that the pottery types may represent ceremonial types common to the local area, so he predicts
they will be found in future excavations of kivas and possibly in
cemeteries at contemporary sites in the area.

The palynological studies are also pertinent to implication
number 12 and give support to it. There are greater concentrations of pollen of *Ephedra* (Mormon tea) and *Erigonum* (buck-
wheat) in the special rooms than in the other rooms at the site.

Both plants are known historically to have had ceremonial and medicinal uses among the Hopi and Zuñi.

I_{16}. To check this implication it is necessary to utilize artifacts which can be presumed to be male-specific or female-specific. These include the following items:

Male-Associated Artifacts	Female-Associated Artifacts
Projectile points	Metates
Arrowshaft tools	Manos
Antler-flakers	Worked sherds
Cores	
Hammerstones	
(Hill 1968: 133)	

By comparing this list with Table 2.1, one can see that the proposition is confirmed.

The three female-associated items were found predominantly in the large rooms, and not in the special rooms; the male-associated items (except for arrowshaft tools) were strongly represented in both large and special rooms; both sets of items were found to some degree in the small rooms—although rarely in significant quantities. The important point, however, is that female-associated items were not significantly present in the special rooms; among all four of these rooms there was only one metate, one mano, and one worked sherd. This lends strong support to the idea that these rooms were generally restricted to males, as was seen to be the case among the present-day western Pueblos.

In summary, it is clear that twelve of the sixteen propositions are unequivocally confirmed (1–8, 11, 13, 14, and 16); two of them (10 and 12) are at least partially confirmed; and only two of them were not confirmed (9 and 15). It is thus demonstrated that the three major room types at Broken K Pueblo were the general functional equivalents of the three major kinds of rooms in present-day Pueblo villages; they may legitimately be called habitation, storage, and ceremonial rooms (or kivas) (Hill 1968: 134).

ADEQUATE CONFIRMATION

A very important question that we have referred to only briefly is that of adequate confirmation: When is a hypothesis adequately confirmed? This is an area of considerable discussion and disagreement in all fields which lack consensus as to ultimate goals and how to design, carry out, and assess research directed toward those goals. There is, at the moment, no such consensus among all archeologists (or among all anthropologists or all social scientists). Even among scientifically oriented archeologists, there is considerable uncertainty as to the nature of and amount of confirmation necessary to establish a hypothesis as a lawlike generalization or general law. This uncertainty will gradually disappear if archeology continues to develop as a scientific discipline because its practitioners—in continuous dialogue with each other—will hammer out the consensus referred to above, and will come to mutual agreement concerning ultimate goals and the best means of achieving these goals. (The interested reader should refer to T. S. Kuhn's discussion of what he calls the "paradigm" of a scientific discipline [Kuhn 1962]). To hasten the development of such a consensus on methods, scientifically oriented archeologists should include in the reports of their investigations a discussion, not only of their hypotheses but also of what they consider to be adequate confirmation of these hypotheses.

A related—and even more basic—point is that of what generalizations concerning human behavior and culture process need to be tested by archeologists, and which generalizations can be accepted without testing as basic operating assumptions. For example, Longacre bases his explanation (p. 35) on the assumption, treated as a general law, that women living in a matrilocal society will learn and pass down female skills, such as pottery manufacture, within the context of the matrilocal residence unit.

As we have stated, the general law used in any explanation must be a previously confirmed law, and the assumption on which Longacre bases his explanation is not a confirmed law. However, archeologists operate in an area that has few confirmed laws. This situation is not unique to archeology, but is a result of its immaturity as a scientific pursuit. In other fields where scientific procedures are followed, the practitioners have, in the past, arrived at a common understanding of what kinds of lawlike generalizations should be accepted without testing as basic assumptions, and what kinds of lawlike generalizations should be subjected to testing (see R. Watson N. D.). This understanding is part of the consensus or conceptual framework referred to in Chapter 1 (see also pp. 150–52), which must be worked out by archeologists who wish to place their discipline on a solid scientific basis. Just as Hill has established a position from which discussion of adequate confirmation can begin, so Longacre has established a position from which discussion can begin on the important topic of what generalizations are to be accepted as basic operating assumptions and what are to be subjected to testing. Debate and discussion of both issues are essential to the establishing of a conceptual framework for an explicitly scientific archeology.

Longacre does not discuss what he regards as adequate confirmation; however, Hill does give some attention to this problem. In the Hill study we have an example of hypothesis confirmation which would without doubt be accepted as valid by all interested archeologists. Yet four of the sixteen implications are not upheld (we referred in detail to only two). Given the hypothetico-deductive framework described in the first part of this chapter, if 25% of Hill's implications are disconfirmed, does that mean the hypothetical law is disconfirmed? Yes, *if* the disconfirmed implications really do follow necessarily from the hypothetical law in the given situation and *if* they really are disconfirmed. However, when dealing with archeological data we cannot always be certain which implications follow. For instance, with respect to Hill's implication number 9 (pp. 40, 42–43, above), because the large jars were not in the excavated storage rooms does not mean they never had been in the storage rooms. There are various ways of accounting for their absence. In fact, negative results from the checking of an implication may indicate interesting and significant lines for research. Hill presents a good discussion of this in the last few pages of his paper:

. . . the propositions that were not confirmed are just as important as the ones that were. . . . In addition to providing evidence of culture-change, they provide new information that cannot be obtained from ethnographic materials. They raise new questions, and provide information which can serve as a basis for generating additional testable propositions. . . . In addition to the fact that new propositions can be generated on the basis of those propositions that were not confirmed, they can also be generated on the basis of information gained in the process of confirming the others. It was suggested, for example, that the apparently paired groups of rooms at the site probably represent the loci of individual household units. This proposition can be tested, of course, by examining the ethnographic evidence to discover the kinds of stylistic differences that distinguish present-day pueblo households and then examining the archeological data in an effort to confirm the presence of similar stylistic variation. One would not even think of gathering data relevant to such a problem unless the problem had been in mind prior to excavation. . . . The number of testable propositions that can be generated with respect to past human behavior is virtually endless. The major conclusion to be drawn is that by using this approach of generating and testing propositions it should be possible to expand our knowledge of the past almost indefinitely. There is no need to rely solely on ethnographic data in making inferences about the past. Although ethnographic evidence can profitably be used to generate propositions, as has been done here, it is equally feasible to use archeological data in the same way. Actually, it matters little what kind of information is used; if the propositions are testable (and of some scientific importance), they are useful to the advancement of knowledge.

It cannot be stressed strongly enough, however, that our propositions must be tested with data that is independent of the data used in formulating them. The most common approach to making inferences

about the past can be illustrated with an example of the way in which
the functions of prehistoric pueblo rooms are usually inferred:

1. The premise is stated that certain rooms look like living
rooms because they contain firepits and mealing bins.

2. Ethnographic data indicate that present-day pueblo living
rooms also contain these features.

3. It is then proposed that since the prehistoric rooms have these
features, they must in fact be functionally the same as the historically
recorded living rooms.

This is reasonable, of course, as far as it goes; but the analysis frequently stops at this point, and the proposition . . . is represented as
fact. In essence, the proposition is generated using both ethnographic
and archeological evidence, but it is left untested; there is little attempt to find independent evidence that would either support or refute
it. This situation is common in all of the social sciences . . . I have
attempted to illustrate that we need not stop with the statement of
propositions; it is nearly always possible to find independent data with
which to test them (Hill 1968: 137–39).

The preceding discussion centers on a topic of considerable
importance to archeologists: the use of ethnographic analogy.

ETHNOGRAPHIC ANALOGY

Theoretical considerations underlying the use of ethnographic
analogy in archeological interpretation have received a good deal
of attention over the past ten years (Ascher 1961, 1962; L. Binford 1967a, 1967b, 1968d; Chang 1967; Freeman 1968; Gould
1968; Thompson 1958). Use of ethnographic analogy and of imitative experiments (knapping flint tools oneself, for instance, or
making experimental pots) implies a uniformitarian view of the
behavior of natural raw materials and of human beings. That is,
one must believe that raw materials and—at least so long as we
are dealing with anatomically modern man—human behavior in
the past are directly comparable to those of the present. More specifically, with respect to human behavior, one must hold that the

types of processes operating within and between human societies now are the same as those operative in the past. Hence, one can observe behavior in the present (the manufacture of stone tools or of certain kinds of pottery, or the manner in which relationships between individual human beings or between human groups of various kinds are expressed in the nature and distribution of material remains made and used by them) and can discover and confirm general laws describing these relationships. Hypothetical laws can also be suggested and tested by archeological or by sociological or other data, or by a combination of them, and can then be applied in explanation of newly accumulated archeological data.

There must have been past forms or patterns of behavior which no longer exist anywhere in the world, but they will be derivable from knowledge of the evidence for them (archeological or historical data) plus knowledge of relevant general laws.

In general discussions of ethnographic analogy, a distinction is frequently made between two kinds of analogy: the "folk-culture," or direct historical approach, and the general comparative approach. The former is well illustrated by [J. G. D.] Clark (1952), and by Anderson (1969) (see also P. J. Watson 1966). The direct-historical approach is applicable in a geographic area like southwest Asia or in some parts of Meso-america, where cultural continuity is strong and where various basic techniques and implements have been practiced and produced for hundreds or even thousands of years. An archeologist working in such an area can take advantage of this fact and gather detailed information in contemporary communities about such practices or implements as are important to him.

However, ethnographic information gathered anywhere, even from historical sources, can be used as an aid in archeological interpretation anywhere in the world. The logical framework for application of both kinds of analogy remains exactly the same: regardless of their source, unless it is agreed that they can be accepted as basic assumptions without need for testing, the proposed analogies are simply hypotheses. As such they must be tested against independent archeological data or against a combination of independent archeological and ethnographic data before they can be accepted. As Hill shows in the preceding example (pp. 37ff.), the testing procedure is the same as with any hypothesis: Implications are deduced from it and these are checked against independent evidence.

This procedure contrasts with the traditional one in that the proposed analogy is not simply suggested and then adopted, but implications are deduced from it and these are checked against independent evidence. Ascher, operating within a traditionalistic framework and with reference to the general comparative approach, has made considerable efforts to define criteria distinguishing justifiable from unjustifiable use of analogy. He states that:

In effect, the new analogy consists of boundary conditions for the choice of suitable analogs. . . . In summary, then, the canon is: seek analogies in cultures which manipulate similar environments in similar ways (Ascher 1961: 319).

It is certainly true that following such a canon will guide the investigator to that ethnographic data which is the richest source of hypotheses for him, but the method of testing must still be a deductive one. It does not matter where the hypothesis comes from (or, in this case, the ethnographic analogy); what matters is whether it is adequately confirmed by appropriate tests, as in the Hill study.

GENERAL LAWS

The logical structure of methodology required by scientific or "new" archeology should now be clear, as well as the manner in which basic epistemological issues are met: Knowledge of the World, Truth, and Explanation. We now come to the topic that represents an important goal of scientific archeology, as indeed it must for all the social sciences, the formulation and testing of hypothetical laws of human behavior and culture process.

Archeologists constantly operate with many kinds of general laws (for example, those having to do with stratigraphy and sedimentation), or with plausible statements in the form of lawlike generalizations (for example, similarity in form means similarity in function and/or chronological proximity), but only recently have archeologists explicitly turned to the task of formulating and testing not only these general laws but also others of significance to the entire field of anthropology.

. . . we all want our discipline to contribute to the knowledge of laws of human behavior. One of the easiest ways that this can be done is to demonstrate the empirical validity of the regularities we think exist. . . . In the past archaeologists have felt bound by the explanations which their data "suggested." The explanatory approach removes this restriction. But it forces the anthropologist to justify the explanations which he chooses to test as being valuable uses of research time. In the long run this obligation can be met only by taking as explanations to be tested problems which are relevant not only to archaeologists but to social science as a whole. Archaeologists claim to have a set of data which is of unique value in studying processes of long term change and development. Yet, we have rarely used our data to do this. Given the freedom to choose explanations for testing, we have incurred the obligation to strive to be relevant (Fritz and Plog 1970: 411–12).

So far very little has been published along these lines, but we can refer to a brief article by Mark P. Leone as an example (Leone 1968). He postulates the hypothetical law that "increasing dependence on agriculture leads to increasing social distance between the minimal economic units needed to make agriculture a successful economic base." He measures social distance in terms of the variability of ceramic styles within a prehistoric village. He infers that this reflects the relative degrees of exogamy and endogamy within these communities. The actual pottery used came from eleven sites in Hay Hollow Valley, ranging from A.D. 400 to 1300 in time (the chronology is based on tree-ring dating). The basic assumption is similar to that of Longacre and Hill (suggested by Deetz in 1960), that pottery is made by the women who teach their daughters and granddaughters, so this knowledge is passed on in the female line. Thus:

. . . we know the women were localized if their craft products were localized. . . . Further, if females were recruited to a village from outside, they would bring to any given village a series of style traditions which would make that village's pottery more variable than it would be if all the wives in a village were born and enculturated within its limits. Hence, the more variable ceramic styles in a village were, whether these are measured by color variation or by design elements on painted pottery . . . , the more exogamous a village was. Conversely, the less variation in female-produced goods in a village, the more endogamous the village was. . . . (Leone 1968: 1150).

The data Leone uses to measure changing dependence on agriculture come from the Reserve area in western New Mexico. He infers further that increased dependence on agriculture (and consequently less dependence on hunting-gathering) should produce different patterns of variability in the respective tool kits. Leone and his associates then quantify and graph this variability for manos, projectile points, and scrapers at a series of sites ranging from 300 B.C. to A.D. 1300 in time. When ceramic variability for the Hay Hollow sites is similarly computed and graphed, the two lines are found to co-vary. Leone concludes: "These nearly simultaneous fluctuations substantiate the hypothesis that as agriculture becomes a greater part of the economic base, village endogamy increases." Thus for this one test case his hypothetical law is confirmed insofar as his quantification procedures are valid and accurate. However, there is certainly considerable ground for further checking before acceptance.

SEEKING BEHAVIORAL CORRELATES
FOR MATERIAL CULTURE

Longacre's study illustrates the testing of a hypothetical explanation he wishes to apply to the archeological data from Carter Ranch Pueblo. In the course of testing the explanation, which involves the residence behavior of the ancient population, he must work out connecting links between his archeological materials and their distributions (potsherds, burials, and so on) on the one hand and the patterned behavior of the prehistoric people who manufactured them on the other. That is, his first task is to operationalize his theoretical framework so that he can relate his hypothesis to the actual pottery, fragmentary architecture, burials, and other archeological remains of the ancient pueblo (see discussion on pp. 34–37 above). He must be able to translate the nature and distribution of cultural debris into the behavior of the prehistoric people responsible for it.

Hill's work illustrates the testing of a hypothetical law to be applied to his archeological data: If the forms of rooms in the prehistoric pueblo are the same as those of modern pueblos, the functions are also the same. He demonstrates the similarity in form, then deduces test implications to check the hypothetical lawlike relationship between form and function in the specified circumstances. In order to carry out the testing he, like Longacre, must arrive at means to translate the nature and distribution of archeological remains into behavior patterns of the prehistoric population. Hence, he deduces test implications designed to enable him to do this.

Robert Whallon is also concerned with this important problem of establishing relationships between various characteristics of the materials preserved in the archeological record and "the structure of the sociocultural systems within which these items were produced and in which they found their function" (Whallon 1968: 223). He is interested in relationships between stylistic variability (as measured by attribute clustering) and aspects of social organization. He was able to demonstrate (statistically) trends in attribute clustering for which he suggests possible explanations based on ethnographic information concerning social and political organization and demography. His measurements of stylistic variability in rim sherds are—like Deetz and Longacre's pottery studies— meant to elicit crucial aspects of socio-political organization from the archeological record.

Another study, that of Dethlefsen and Deetz (1966), illustrates a means of testing directly some of the possible relationships between material objects and human behavior. The specific problem they are attacking is one fundamental to all archeology: how to arrive at a relative chronological placement for a series of sites or assemblages. The process usually used is referred to as seriation. Seriation has been utilized on a wide range of problems and types of assemblages from Upper Paleolithic end scrapers to Bronze Age cemeteries. Most frequently it has been applied to pottery, especially by Ford (for instance, Ford 1949). Use of frequency seriation involves two assumptions: (1) Artifact types are continuously distributed and change gradually through time. Any particular type begins as a minor component of the total assemblage, then becomes popular, and slowly dies out. The most common graphical representation of this development is the so-called battleship-shaped curve (Ford 1962). (2) Sites most similar in type frequencies are closest in time.

Dethlefsen and Deetz became interested in testing these assumptions concerning stylistic change. In order to do this they needed artifact assemblages of known absolute chronological relationships. The artifacts they chose are New England gravestones made between 1680 and 1820. These tombstones are ideal for a number of reasons: (1) Each stone carries its own date. (2) Relevant cultural information such as status and kinship of the individual is recorded on the stones. (3) Historical documents relating to the tombstones are available. (4) The stones have a wide geographic spread.

Dethlefsen and Deetz collected tombstone data from many New England cemeteries and tabulated the relative frequency of each of the three basic stone motifs—death's heads, cherub, or urn-and-willow—by decade. The graphs of these relative frequencies do have the form of battleship-shaped curves. Thus, in this well-controlled case they have confirmed the first basic assumptions of seriation. In addition, by computing the relative frequencies for each cemetery separately, they have been able to determine the diffusion rates for these motifs and the manner in which seriation graphs are distorted if data from sites far distant from each other are plotted (Deetz and Dethlefsen 1965). Because these data were collected from only one set of artifacts, Deetz and Dethlefsen's conclusions cannot be considered as confirmed general laws of stylistic change, but they do provide a beginning for the confirmation of such laws.

SUMMARY

In Chapters 1 and 2 we describe the logical structure of scientific archeology, which is the same as that of all science. Examples from recent archeological writing illustrate the basic points of this structure. Some archeologists are avowedly intent on formulating and testing a variety of hypothetical explanations and general laws, some to be used explicitly for archeological explanation, and some to be used within the wider realm of social science to explain and to predict human (cultural) behavior. Such archeologists do not wish to rely on plausible but untested hypotheses concerning culture process (as shown by the Maya invasion controversy) or on plausible but untested inferences drawn from ethnographic data as a means of interpreting it (as shown by the Hill example).

They insist upon subjecting hypothetical laws and explanations to tests designed to confirm or disconfirm them, because only the confirmed hypothesis should have a place in the body of established archeological or social scientific theory.

Part Two

Explanatory Frameworks
for Archeology: Systems Theory
and the Ecological Approach

🏮🏮

CHAPTER THREE

THE NORMATIVE VIEW OF CULTURE
AND THE SYSTEMS THEORY APPROACH

THE METHODS AND THEORY of any discipline must be attuned to its subject matter. Field research designs, analytical procedures, and interpretive frameworks should reflect the researcher's conception of archeology and its central theme—culture. If archeologists are to develop a rigorously scientific approach they must treat culture in a scientific manner. Whether archeologists can adopt the methods necessary for scientific research depends largely on their definition of culture and the conceptual framework with which the archeological researcher approaches his data. The definition of culture that has usually been employed by ethnographers and is, implicitly or explicitly, used by most archeologists is termed (by its critics) the "normative view of culture." Flannery asserts that practitioners who hold the normative view, "treat culture as a body of shared ideas, values and beliefs—the 'norms' of a human group" (1967: 119). L. Binford considers that "a normative theorist is one who sees as his field of study the ideational basis for varying ways of human life—culture. . . . The archaeologist's task then lies in abstracting from cultural products the normative concepts extant in the minds of men now dead" (1965:203). These normative concepts, or "mental templates" as they are often called, served as models for the prehistoric man who made the ar-

tifact (see Chapter 5, pp. 131–32). It is assumed that the archeologist's task is to discover inductively the ideas that governed the
production of the artifact, and in this way to get at the essence of
the culture.

Struever points out that:

It is the description of change in these shared ideas through time and
space—as expressed in the material culture he excavates—that
becomes the normative archeologist's major objective. He attempts
to reconstruct prehistoric cultures in terms of a series of normative
concepts expressed in a list of typical artifact, feature, and even settlement forms (1971: 10).

Because artifacts and other archeological remains are conceived of as representing their manufacturers' ideas, they also reflect the shared ideas that comprise the extinct culture. If the normative archeologist has been able to "abstract" the idea or
template behind the artifact, then he considers that he has determined an aspect or conceptual building block of the culture in
question. A series of templates or, in reality, artifact types are
considered to add up to the sum of the culture, or at least to be a
reflection of it.

This building block, or partitive approach, to culture is very
convenient for archeologists attempting to measure the "similarity" between cultures, because one can simply tabulate the total
shared artifact types for any two sites and thus supposedly determine how many ideas or norms the two cultures hold in common.

This emphasis on artifacts as reflections of shared ideas as
the essence of the culture has led to the incorporation of the concept of type sites, with typical assemblages and typical features.
Consequently, when a normative archeologist excavates a single
site, he may consider it as typifying all sites of that period and region. Concern with type collections and typical sites results in the
ignoring of a great deal of variation that is actually present in archeological material. The normative definition of culture, center-

ing on shared ideas and reconstructed templates treated in a partitive manner, has resulted in a crisis in archeological interpretation. Final recourse, in formulating explanations, must be to historical accidents, such as migration and diffusion, or to what Binford calls "paleopsychology." This is because normativists do not deal with relationships between norms but attempt to explain the norms themselves. However, because these norms are regarded as independent forms and not as functional aspects of the culture, one can only describe them and their travels or distributions. These descriptions provide little information about the archeological remains which would enable us to test processual hypotheses concerning the extinct culture.

THE SYSTEMIC VIEW OF CULTURE

Because it is impossible to observe directly what people were thinking, research hypotheses and models must be testable against the observable behavior of these people. For archeologists, behavior is observable in the material remains of the culture. Realization of this has led many archeologists away from the normative view of culture that depends on mental templates and shared ideas, values, and norms. These archeologists have replaced dependence on cognitive explanation with a focus on material remains viewed as a reflection of past behavioral patterns. The logical result of this position is the conviction that one of the major aims of archeology must be to correlate the structure of material remains with the behavioral elements of a cultural system.

Some archeologists are attempting to formulate explanations of cultural processes which can be tested by the form and disposition of material remains in the archeological record (see Chapter 2).

Lewis R. Binford (following Aberle 1960 and White 1959: 8) states that:

. . . in our definition, culture is not necessarily shared; it is participated in. And it is participated in differentially.

. . . culture is an extrasomatic adaptive system that is employed in
the integration of a society with its environment and with other sociocultural systems (Binford 1965: 205).

Kent V. Flannery suggests that we study this complex of systems
by attempting to isolate and examine each of the constituent subsystems as a separate variable and then recombining (1967:120).
The advantage of this "systemic" approach to culture is not that it
is necessarily a more accurate representation of reality, but that
considering the nature of archeological evidence and investigation,
it will lead to more productive models, that is, those which lead to
testable hypotheses involving as many categories of evidence as
possible. A normative approach to culture results in the utilization
of techniques that assume similarities in cultures can be expressed
in terms of a single variable (see also Chapter 5, pp. 119–20). An
example is the lumping of all ceramic variations into one measure
of chronological proximity while ignoring other possible causes of
variation (Ford 1962). Such a lumping assumes that ceramic variability is caused solely by change through time, not by geographic
distance between settlements, or different social groups within a
single settlement, or functional differences between human groups
within a community. Lumping these possible causes of variation
under a heading of chronology is an oversimplification.

A contrary view is stated by Binford:

Culture is not a univariate phenomenon, nor is its functioning to be
understood or measured in terms of a single variable—the spatial-temporal transmission of ideas. On the contrary, culture is multivariate,
and its operation is to be understood in terms of many causally relevant variables which may function independently or in varying combinations. It is our task to isolate these causative factors and to seek reg-
ular, statable, and predictable relationships between them (L. Binford 1965: 205).

There is a shift from exclusive concern with entities to interest in
the relations between and among groups and entities. An archeol-

ogist interested in such relations (possible laws of cultural process) cannot search for the "typical" site and stop there; he must attempt to discover the range of variation in the prehistoric record and to interrelate the causal variables which resulted in its present form.

For the systemic theorist, culture is made up of parts, structurally different from each other, but articulated within the total system. More broadly, culture and its environments represent a number of articulated systems in which change occurs through a series of minor, linked variations in one or more of these systems. A major objective of archeology is to understand the linkages between parts in both the cultural and environmental systems as reflected in the archeological data (Struever 1971:10).

It is this systemic view of culture with its multivariate approach and emphasis on relationships and variability that should be the interpretive framework of scientifically oriented archeology.

SYSTEMS THEORY

There is available to archeologists an already productive framework for analyzing systems developed by a group of researchers known as general systems theorists. One of the originators of this emerging discipline is Ludwig von Bertalanffy, who conceived of a developing embryo as a system of interacting parts that had an inertia and regulating mechanisms of its own (1950). Several other social and physical scientists formulated parallel schemes for interpreting various phenomena in the organismic, physical, and cultural realms (Von Neumann and Morgenstern 1947, Rapoport 1953, Ashby 1956, Wiener 1954, and Boulding 1956). Their basic assumption is that there are "systems so basic in nature that they can be seen operating in virtually every field" (Flannery 1967: 122). These underlying "rules" which seem to govern the behavior of entities so diverse as a digital computer, living organism, or a socio-cultural system are more than simple analogies. Delineating the similarities among these different kinds of systems is considered to be a form of generalizing or of abstracting basic realities (Buckley 1968: 509).

General systems theory seeks a body of systematic theoretical constructs which is concerned with the general relationships in the empirical world (Boulding 1956). Insights into basic systems that have been derived from and tested on other bodies of data by general systems theorists can be usefully applied to prehistoric cultural systems by archeologists. This framework was developed for disciplines which, like archeology, are limited to the method of controlled observations in seeking testable probabilistic laws.

Archeologists have developed few unifying theories of cultural behavior that can be employed as interpretive frameworks. The two basic models that have been utilized in anthropology and sociology, and implicitly in archeology, are the "mechanistic" and the "organismic functional" theories of cultural systems. We believe these types of models are insufficient for dealing with the complex nature of sociocultural processes, and that a framework utilizing elements of the general systems approach is more appropriate.

The mechanistic model has been borrowed from engineering and treats culture as a "machine" in which the output always bears a particular relation to the input. This relation is determined by the "rules" of the machine or system. This interpretive framework is useful for the simplest of processes, such as: An increase in the presence of warfare in a region leads to an increase in the construction of defenses. The various parts of a mechanistic system work together in harmony to produce the predicted results. Because no allowance is made for change or dynamic regulation in the face of adversity, the mechanistic model is inadequate for a study of culture process.

The organismic or functional model has been borrowed from biology and has proved useful in many situations. The basic concept is that each element of the system is interdependent, works together, and functions to maintain the operation of the total system. Organisms grow and develop according to a predetermined plan. An organism is able to adapt to certain changes in the input from its physical surroundings by employing sensing and regulating devices within its system. Although an organism is capable of adapting to change, this change must be within limited boundaries. The condition of the organism's system must remain very close to a predetermined state. Successful adaptation means the organism alters its interaction with the environment in order to maintain its original form in a milieu of changing surroundings. The important variables in an organismic model are those determining the entity's viable state or structure, and the manner in which each part functions within the whole.

This framework has proved to be very useful in interpreting data from systems that are not changing significantly, and in understanding how parts of systems work together to adapt to small changes in the environment. As an example, increased warfare in a region could be considered from the perspective of an organismic model. Plausible responses expected by the investigator might then include the increase of its outer shell (defenses), movement to another environment (resettlement), or even development of a new element (such as a strong army of its own) to maintain its static state.

These "responses" cover a certain range of reality, but by no means all the possible alternatives open to a sociocultural system. The utilization of the organismic approach has led to a greater dependence on classification and categorization in the traditional biological and cultural sciences than has the deductive approach of the physicist, which involves working from confirmed general laws and deducing test implications to test hypothetical explanations. A framework that emphasizes the ubiquity of a system's structure will naturally lead to concentration on taxonomies and on goal-oriented (teleological) explanations of growth and development (Rapoport and Horvath 1959).

Some archeologists believe it is possible for their discipline to move beyond the formulation of taxonomies and teleological explanations. Society, or past sociocultural systems, should not be conceived of as mechanical or organismic systems, but, as Buckley suggests, as complex adaptive systems (1968). The promise of the systems approach is that it will enable archeologists to get at the full complexity of the interacting phenomena of cultural process. The basic assumption of this approach is that the great complexity of these systems and processes is organized and potentially understandable.

General systems theory seeks to classify systems according to the way their components are organized and interrelated, and to derive the laws or typical patterns of behavior for the different classes of systems (Rapoport 1968). Over the past twenty-five years this goal has been partially realized through the work of a number of researchers. There is already a voluminous body of literature and laws concerning the nature of systems and processes which is available for application to the archeological record. One of the originators of general systems theory, Von Bertalanffy, suggests that the ultimate justification for this change in general frame of reference is in the specific achievements which would not have been possible without the new theory (1962).

The method of the physical sciences is to attempt to understand a complexity by examining its constituent parts and trying to build up a working system by "superimposing" these constituent parts (Rapoport and Horvath 1959). This method has been so widely utilized that it has become synonymous with the word "analysis." W. Ross Ashby, a systems theorist, warns us not to approach a complex system by this method:

. . . for this process gives us only a vast number of separate parts or items of information, the results of whose interactions no one can predict. If we take such a system to pieces, we find that we cannot reassemble it (as quoted by Buckley 1967: 39).

The classical model of the additive nature of a system's parts is useful in some situations, but not when applied to cultural systems. For these systems, the whole is equal to more than the sum of its parts. The properties of members of a system must be measured in terms of themselves and of the system as a whole. This holistic, systemic framework necessitates a shift away from a concern with "substance" and toward a focus on relations between the components of a system. The systems-oriented archeologist should not be interested in artifacts or activities in themselves, but should seek out their internal relations within a system and work out the way this system behaves in a given environment. The traditional analytic technique for studying relationships has been to isolate pairs of variables and to study their behavior. This technique is no longer regarded as adequate because in most systems, pairs of variables do not act in isolation nor do they perform a constant task.

The analytic reductionist approach has also proven inadequate in face of the increasing number of variables found relevant to cultural processes. Studying the reaction of each pair of variables in each state of a system may be possible in small, simple processes, but as soon as a system reaches a complexity where the components no longer act in a sequential or linear fashion, then the mathematics and investigation required become overwhelming. Theoretical reservations and practical limitations make the study of complex systems by traditional reductionist methods an unrealistic procedure. Processes and systems should no longer be considered simple until proven otherwise. Systems theorists have replaced that dictum with another, *"Systems explanations are complex until proven otherwise."* Occam's Razor can be applied to determine the best explanation only when both possibilities predict the results equally well, but simplicity cannot be condoned in the face of inaccuracy.

SYSTEMS TERMINOLOGY

One needs an introduction to some of the basic terms and concepts utilized by systems theorists in order to grasp the ways in which they have been and could be applied to archeological research.

A whole which functions as a whole by virtue of the interdependence of its parts is called a *system* (Rapoport 1968:*xvii*).

A system is a set of objects together with *relationships* between the objects and between their *attributes* (Hall and Fagen 1956: 18).

Hall and Fagen go on to say that their definition implies that a system also has properties, functions, or purposes distinct from its constituent objects, relationships, and attributes (1956). The attributes are measureable properties of the objects. The relationships can be of varying degrees of complexity and the precise relationships to be considered in the context of a given set of objects depends on the research problem at hand.

This emphasis leads to a concern for explaining and describing the structure of a system, but "a system as a continuous, boundary-maintaining, variously related assemblage of parts, is not to be confused with the structure or organization its components may take on at any particular time" (Buckley 1967:5). The criterion of classification of a system should not be its structure at any one point in time because this is a temporary condition. The unit of dynamic-processual analysis should be the systemic matrix of interacting, goal-seeking, decision-making individuals and subgroups. Ashby suggests that the analysis of a system not be based on materials or energy, but on the regularity of behavior. To him a dynamic system is one in which its internal state, and the state of its surroundings, defines uniquely the next state it will attain (Ashby 1962). It is possible for an entity to change its structure and outward appearance without losing its identity.

It is this addition of structure-changing and structure-elaborating features to already utilized structure-maintaining features of inherently unstable systems that makes systems theory relevant to the study of prehistoric cultures. Returning, for example, to the settlement in a region of increasing warfare, we see that various changes of structure would help adapt an endangered settlement to this particular situation. For instance, a generally sedentary agricultural community could become semisedentary and rely on pastoralist pursuits in marginal areas to avoid the dangers of organized warfare.

The environment of a given system is the set of all objects that directly affect the system or are affected by the system. The environment can include climate, topography, natural resources, food sources, other social groups, and other influences external to the system itself. Whether something belongs to the system or to the environment is a decision that depends on the interests of the researcher. To define the environment of a system one must determine how and where it interacts with the environment.

Systems theorists recognize that culture and environment are not mutually exclusive systems and postulate the interrelation of the cultural and environmental systems (see Chapter 4 on the ecological view of culture as used by archeologists). The viability of a system depends to a great extent on its ability to react to the relevant properties of its environment and to adjust its structure accordingly.

Persistence or continuity of an adaptive system may require, as a necessary condition, change in its structure, the degree of change being a complex function of the internal state of the system, the state of its relevant environment, and the nature of the interchange between the two (Buckley 1968:493).

This ability of an organism or system to read or interpret its surroundings is referred to as mapping. A system maps or transmits the set of information from its environment into the system, which is composed of structural alternatives. This mapping is seldom complete, and the problems of information flow and means of communication have given rise to information theory, a new subdiscipline within systems theory (see p. 86 of this chapter and Rapoport 1956).

The differentiation between a closed and an open system is important to understanding the dynamics of systems theory. A system is closed if there is no import or export of energy in any of its forms (Hall and Fagen 1956). Conversely, in an open system the interchange of energy and information with the environment is an essential factor. Whether a system is considered open or closed depends on how much of the universe is included, by definition, in the system and how much in the environment.

In order to deal analytically with a system, it is necessary to recognize the types of processes that govern it. Stable equilibrium is a state in which a small change in the system will be counteracted, and the system will return to its original stable state. Unstable equilibrium is a situation where a small perturbation or displacement can lead to a great change in the state of a system, or even to a restructuring of its components. There is a continuum of types of equilibrium between these two extremes. Most stable equilibrial systems are closed and have no interchange with their environments. They characteristically use up their excess energy and reach a state of final stability.

Open systems depend intimately on the exchange of energy and information with their environment. The process that works in open systems to maintain their structure within certain limits in the face of a changing environment is called homeostasis. Homeostasis depends on the ability of self-regulating devices to maintain the system in a compatible manner with its surroundings. The structure of these systems is never self-maintaining; a constant expenditure of energy of some kind is required to maintain any open system's steady state (Buckley 1967: 130). Orderliness and organization are the opposite of entropy or disorder, which always continue to increase in the world. The complex system maintains its high level of organization by continually "sucking" orderliness from its environment in the form of organic foods.[1] Thus, the open

[1] Although the logical extension of this concept to forms of social organization has not yet been made, it is probably true that the law of increasing entropy or disorder could yield some interesting insights into the development of "organized" urban society, viewed as feeding upon the breakdown

system of an animal or society, which seemingly breaks the law of increasing entropy when viewed as an isolated closed system, actually fits very well into this principle if the total environment of the open system is taken into account.

Both equilibrial and homeostatic mechanisms are concerned with maintaining the structure of a system. Prehistoric cultural systems not only maintained themselves but also changed their structures and systems. It is this process of change that systems-oriented archeologists attempt to discover and explain.

Systems theorists have invented a new term, "morphogenesis," to express not only structure-maintaining features but also the structure-elaborating and changing features of the inherently dynamic, complex, adaptive system (Buckley 1967: 14). Buckley attempts to clarify the difference between structure-maintaining and structure-changing features by suggesting that the former involves a homeostatic process in socio-cultural systems while societal change is a morphogenic process (1967: 58).

An important part of this discussion is concerned with interdependence of a system's components and its ability to react to its environment and regulate its processes. All of these relations in both homeostatic and morphogenic systems are based on some form of feedback. These systems have the property of feeding back a portion of their outputs or behavior into the input in such a way as to affect succeeding outputs (see Fig. III-1). Thus the output of a system is modified by the error between its previous output and some preset goal (Rapoport and Horvath 1959).

The study of feedback systems is known as cybernetics, the science of communication and control. Cybernetics examines patterns of signals which transmit information within a system and from one system to another (Rapoport 1968:*xix*). Maruyama (1963) differentiates between two divisions of cybernetics which involve negative and positive types of feedback. The first division

---

of former types of organization, such as family structure, interpersonal relationships, and so on.

of cybernetics is the science of self-regulating and equilibrating systems. These systems have incorporated negative feedback cycles to keep their states stable and within certain bounds.

Figure III-1 illustrates a simple feedback system. An input or stimulus is received from the environment and affects the system. The system produces an output that is in some way related to the input, and to the relations and rules of the system. The nature and magnitude of this output is sensed by the receptor part of the system and its regulating devices modify the system's treatment of future input to produce output close to the original state. The method of regulation varies according to the type of system. Examples are the genes of a cell, or the preconceived specifications of the inventor of a machine.

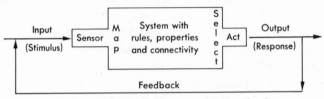

Figure III-1: Simple System with Feedback
(see page 73)

In the cybernetic framework goal-regulated feedback replaces the teleological explanations of the traditional biologists. An example of a negative feedback mechanism is the temperature-regulating thermostat in a house. When the thermostat senses that the temperature is too low, it increases the heat input until the desired goal is attained.

Maruyama considers the second division of cybernetics to be the study of deviation-amplifying and reciprocal-causal relationships (1963). This concept has long been used in the economic literature in discussions of increases in wages and prices during inflationary periods. It is also illustrated by the well-known dictum, "the rich get richer."

Deviation-amplifying or positive feedback mechanisms are characteristic of many adaptive and socio-cultural systems. In contrast to the stabilizing effect of negative feedback, positive feedback mechanisms induce changes of state or structure in morphogenic systems. Most cultural processes in the prehistoric record involve some forms of positive feedback.

Buckley emphasizes the crucial role played by deviation. The system must select and preserve through some form of positive feedback the aspects of this deviation which are favorable to the systemic structure (1968: 495). A social system may be subjected to many small perturbations, but because of the structure of the system only a few will stimulate a positive feedback cycle.

As an example of positive feedback let us re-examine the case of warring settlements in a region. Before organized warfare began let us assume the communities were small, unfortified, and reasonably peaceful. They were in a state of equilibrium, although it may have been somewhat unstable because of pressure on available resources. One night an act of vandalism occurred, a house was burned, or some property was stolen. It was not known who was guilty, but the maligned village sought the support of one of her neighbors and raided the village she distrusted the most. The integrating or homeostatic mechanisms such as treaties, ritual cooperation, or kin relations were not strong enough to keep the system within its bounds. This led to further retaliatory raids that forced the settlements in the region to amalgamate into several larger centers that could be fortified and could support a temporary army. The amalgamation into large settlements caused a concentration in wealth which led to greater temptation for outside attack. This led to the necessity for a permanent army, which resulted in the temptation to use this army in an offensive manner to attack other communities. Thus the cycle of warfare is started and propagates itself in a "vicious spiral." Detailed knowledge concerning the first act of vandalism (where and when it occurred, who did it, and so on) is irrelevant to the understanding of this state of warfare and amalgamation into defensive cities. To understand the process and the state of affairs at any one point in time, one must understand the deviation-amplifying mechanisms that affected this system. It is not necessary to know who or which side fired the first shot at Lexington in 1775 in order to understand why it led to widespread hostilities.

When systems such as those in the preceding examples are in unstable equilibrium, any small incident or perturbation (initial kick) can set a series of deviation-amplifying (positive feedback) mechanisms into action, which may make the situation irreversible. The resulting state may be extremely different from the initial one. The more complex and higher order systems, such as cultural systems, are composed of many feedback loops of different orders, both positive and negative. By means of these feedback loops, the components of the system are able to interpret and respond to various inputs from the environment and from other members of the system.

DESCRIBING SYSTEMS

The state of a system is its current structure in terms of attributes of its components and the nature of its relationships. This means that given an initial state, the path the system takes is uniquely determined (assuming a similar environment), regardless of how the system arrived at the initial state. Thus the relevant effects of a system's history will be manifest in some form in its current state.

The clearest way to represent the state of a system is by means of graphs (Harary, Norman, and Cartwright 1965). Let us assume that the only variables relevant to the system we were discussing previously are the number of people per community, and the percentage of a community under arms (soldiers). A diagram of the various possible states of the system might be represented by Figure III-2. (This is, of course, a simplification of the number of relevant variables.)

Each point on this diagram represents a possible state of the system in terms of these two variables. If the state of the system changes over time (t_0 to t_1), then the vector that connects these two points is the trajectory of this system during the specified time. The state of a system is specified by its position on the graph, and the change in its state is described by the trajectory. The graph can be divided into a number of different sections or regions, each representing a different type of state (for example, peace and warfare). Within each of these regions there is usually

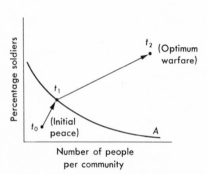
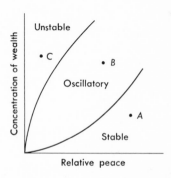

Figure III-2: Graph of Possible States of Peace and War in the System

Figure III-3: Graph of Potential Behavior of the System

one optimum point or state. Each of these regions can be thought of as basins of attraction, and the lines between them as boundaries. Once the trajectory brings a system within a region, there is a natural tendency for that state to move toward this optimum point. The change of a system within one region is usually gradual and not discontinuous, but once it approaches—and as it crosses—a boundary between two regions, this change is normally accelerated and seems discontinuous.

In Figure III-2, the state of the relative hostilities of a system is shown for two equal time periods (t_0 to t_1 and t_1 to t_2, respectively). A moderate increase in the number of people, percentage of soldiers, or various combinations resulting in a position on the graph below line A will leave the system in peace. A negative feedback cycle will ensue, which tends to return the system to position t_0. However, once line A is crossed, a positive feedback cycle will set in that pushes the system toward optimum warfare.

One would construct a gradual function of change for the first time period and a more rapid change for the second time period. The boundary of the basins of attraction (Line A in Fig. III-2) can be considered as a threshold. Near the boundary or threshold a small change in the value of one variable (a small perturbation or initial kick) may place the system's state within another region, which can lead to a great change in the state of the system.

The more abstract variables of a system can also be expressed in graphical form (Fig. III-3). In this example the variables illustrated are the relative peace in a region and the relative concentration of wealth in each community.

The graph represents three types of state of the system: stable, oscillatory, and unstable. The boundary lines would be defined on the basis of empirical investigations. At any point in time the behavior of the system can be found by plotting the values of relative peace and concentration of wealth for the system.

Point A represents a stable state of the system that has high relative peace and low concentration of wealth. The stable state would be characterized by stable conditions in *all* aspects (subsystems) of the system, not only those involving peace and wealth. In other terms there would be strong negative feedback cycles that make it unlikely that the system would change significantly.

Point B represents an oscillatory or variable state of the system. In this case the system has less relative peace and more concentration of wealth than the system of point A. This system would be characterized by significant changes in many aspects of the system in comparison with that at point A, but negative feedback cycles would still tend to keep change from being so great as to destroy the system.

Point C represents an unstable state. In this case the system has little peace and much concentration of wealth. Negative feedback would be weaker and one could expect changes in the system moving it to other unstable states, into an oscillatory state, or even destroying the system altogether.

A change in value of one of the variables can result in a change in the nature of the system's behavior. The relations in this diagram are an expression of the ultimate behavior of the system in structural terms.

It must be made clear that a description of the trajectory of a system is not to be equated with an explanation of the processes involved. The products of an evolutionary or developmental sequence must not be confused with the processes that caused and governed that sequence. One recent example of this is the recently proposed explanation of the downfall of the Maya civilization (Sabloff and Willey 1967; discussed in Chapter 2.). The authors suggested that the primary cause of the Maya collapse was an invasion from outside. However, an invasion is only an event, and even if verified it would not serve as an explanation of the process.

If the state of a system we are studying has been adequately described in terms of its relevant properties, then we should be able to predict in a probabilistic sense the future behavior of the system.

The analysis of a complex system can be demonstrated by taking a simple example and working through the method. The systems theory approach is to treat the entire system in a holistic manner and to sample its structure through controlled investigation. Only rarely is a researcher able to "experiment" with complex systems such as social systems. Consequently use of this method does not require analytic experiments, but relies on multivariate analysis. The most important step in the analysis of a system is formulating a directed graph (or diagraph) of the interrelations of the components in the system. Constructing the graph forces the researcher to make explicit what components influence which other components and in what way (Fig. III-4). These relations or connections can be measured by three different scales of ascending power (see Chapter 5 for discussion of scales of measurement). First, one must determine the direction of the influence; second, he must determine whether this relation is positive or negative; and finally, if possible, he should determine the magnitude of this influence on either an ordinal or an interval scale.

The direction and future behavior of a system can be calculated from a detailed analysis of the directions of influences between components and of the nature of the feedback loops. If one has correctly portrayed the system, then he will be able to predict the future states of the system and thus to test his understanding of the nature of the system. It also makes explicit what types of data and which relations one must study.

Figure III-4 is an oversimplified graph of the warring communities situation we have discussed. The logic and structure of this three-component system are straightforward enough not to necessitate a mathematical approach. The three components are: (1) the relative concentrations of people and wealth per community, (2) the relative agricultural efficiency of the people of this geographical region, and (3) the amount of warfare in this region.

In this situation an increase in the concentration of people and wealth into large communities will increase the amount of warfare, and in turn, an increase in the amount of warfare will force more people to live in the concentrated and defendable centers. These two components influence each other in a positive manner, and the feedback loop between them (loop *A*) is a deviation-amplifying mechanism. If this were the only loop, or the dominant loop, involved in the system, then the instability in the system would continuously increase until the system breaks apart.

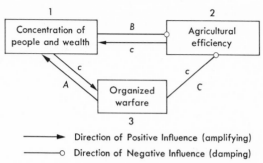

Direction of Positive Influence (amplifying)
Direction of Negative Influence (damping)

Figure III-4: Diagraph of a Cultural System Model

Feedback loop *B* represents an increase in agricultural efficiency which enables a greater concentration of people in the city, but this in turn decreases the general agricultural efficiency because farmers are separated from their land. Thus the total effect of loop *B* is a negative, equilibrating type of mechanism, which alone would lead to a predetermined state of optimum stability. Loop *C* in the system depicts a positive influence of agricultural efficiency on concentration of people and wealth, which has a positive influence on the growth of warfare, but—as just shown—this in turn decreases the agricultural efficiency. Consequently, the total effect of loop *C* is negative or equilibrating.

Because only three components and loops are considered here, we can predict, by inspection, the future behavior of the system. A society or an organism contains many deviation-amplifying loops, as well as deviation-counteracting loops, and an understanding of a society cannot be attained without studying both types of loops and the relationships between them. The action of a system as a whole depends on the strength of each loop and the number of connections among components (Maruyama 1963). If the model were more complex, it would be necessary to utilize matrix algebra to solve this problem. For this example the solution would indicate that the system can either expand and explode or can oscillate between increasing and decreasing amounts of warfare. There are many examples in the culture historical record of systems that have acted in these two ways, and it should be possible by a comparative study of the relevant variables of these societies to determine which values of each relationship are required for each type of behavior. The expression of this model and its solution in graphical and equation form focuses the researcher's attention on crucial relations to be measured in future work, and facilitates quantitative treatment of models of cultural change.

Despite the great promise of systems theory for the interpretation of cultural structures and processes, there has been almost no use of it by archeologists. However, several archeologists have suggested that this is one of the directions archeological research will take (Flannery 1967, Hole and Heizer 1969, Clarke 1968, and Doran 1970). Kent V. Flannery (1968) has published an article that explicitly attempts to utilize various aspects of systems theory to explain a cultural process. He uses an ecosystem model which enables us to see aspects of this prehistoric culture change which are not superficially apparent. He examines the transition from food collecting to sedentary agriculture in terms of a series of "procurement systems" of specific plant and animal genera whose ranges crosscut several environments. His ecosystem model includes many regulatory mechanisms that were imposed on man by nature, such as the seasonality of the wild resources. The model also incorporates the scheduling of the human group's activities which resolved the conflicts between procurement systems.

Flannery describes seven procurement systems, and focuses attention on a relatively minor source of food during the food-collecting era, "Wild Grass Procurement." Although these plants began as minor parts of the diet, random variations in the genetic makeup of one of the species, maize, initiated the deviation-amplifying, positive feedback cycle which enabled these plants to increase in importance. The genetic changes made maize and, in a similar way, beans increasingly profitable to harvest and to sow, which led to further favorable changes in their genetic structure.

The scheduling of the planting of these crops in the spring and harvesting in the fall interfered with the normal collection patterns of two other procurement systems. The choice was made to invest time increasingly in maize and bean collection, which increased the peoples' dependence on these two cultivable plants. The system had been set in motion in one direction and did not reach stability again until these two crops were the center of an intensive system of agriculture.

The implications of this approach for the prehistorian are clear: it is vain to hope for the discovery of the first domestic corn cob, the first pottery vessel, the first hieroglyphic, or the first site where some other major breakthrough occurred. Such deviations from the pre-existing pattern almost certainly took place in such a minor and accidental way that their traces are not recoverable. More worthwhile would be an investigation of the mutual causal processes that amplify these tiny deviations into major changes in prehistoric culture (Flannery 1968: 85).

In this article Flannery utilizes some of the concepts of systems theory in a simple and straightforward manner. It is not new to speak of deviation-amplifying mechanisms or of scheduling a community's time. What is unique about this article is that he explicitly asserts a systems approach should be used to understand cultural change and, further, that efforts to explain culture processes should not be aimed primarily at particular events and initial discoveries, but at the causal relations and resulting developments that were involved in making these small perturbations into significant changes.

THE SYSTEMS PERSPECTIVE

The adoption of systems theory as an interpretive and investigatory framework necessitates modifications in the methods of contemporary archeology. Just as the framework through which one views data influences his results, it also dictates his methods. The assumption of system theorists that culture and processes are complex until proven otherwise requires that the collection and analysis of data be done in a manner that emphasizes the variability in the archeological record and attempts to sample its range of variation.

From a systemic view . . . one excavated site represents a single example of one settlement type and does not reflect the whole settlement system. . . . A systemic definition of culture, therefore, imposes a number of data-collecting requirements on the archeologist. If his aim is to describe prehistoric lifeways, his frame of reference must be regional and not the boundaries of a single site (Struever 1971: 11).

In addition to formulating temporal sequences for a region we must investigate the different forms and functions of settlements during each period, as well as their configurations and demographic parameters. Sampling within a site must include all aspects of the site in an attempt to define the range of activities performed there.

Artifacts must be categorized and analyzed in a manner that enables their variability to be compared along many different dimensions (see Chapter 5, pp. 126ff.). Clustering and grouping artifacts into "types" is a useful and necessary procedure for some kinds of analysis, but not for a systemic analysis. It might be better to measure all of the relevant variables of the artifacts and consider the distribution of each of these variables independently before clustering them into types. This gives the researcher more than one dimension along which to measure artifact variability. Binford advocates this type of procedure when he suggests that technical, morphological, and decorative dimensions of artifacts be compared separately (1965).

Various types of multivariate analysis have already been utilized, and further developments in this field promise to facilitate the use of a systems approach (see Chapter 5, and Cowgill 1968).

As we have noted earlier in this chapter a primary goal of

new archeology is to explain archeological data in terms of culture processes. Systems theory is an especially powerful method with which to investigate process, but it also makes several demands on the manner in which we view process. The most important point is that the trajectory, or successive states of a system, is *not* itself the process. In no way can products be equated with process. The process consists of the general rules and specific dynamic relations that act upon the system to produce its trajectory. The method usually utilized by archeologists to describe (or explain) a process is to isolate two or more variables, and to measure their relations over a period of time. This may produce an interesting approximation of a developmental sequence, but will not yield an accurate description of a process. Components of a system should be measured in terms of their own properties and those they derive from the system as a whole. To isolate a variable such as pottery variability or tool heterogeneity from its system and to study its changes over time is not studying a systemic process. These artifacts may reflect the value of a cultural variable, but there is no assurance that they do this equally well during each period or that they maintain their same "position" within the system during each of the periods.

The greatest contribution of systems theory to archeological research is in the formulation of testable models of human behavior. The central purpose of a theoretical model is to aid the researcher in the selection of relevant variables and significant hypotheses from an infinite number of possibilities. This enables him to concentrate his efforts in productive areas of his general problem. The key to the effective formulation of systems models is ability and insight in creating the directed graph representations of cultural systems. These are built up from logical deductions and from data already at hand. They are tested by calculating their future behavior from the equations that express their interconnectivity and then checking these predictions against the empirical situation.

There are several subdisciplines within the general field of systems theory that have aided construction of these models of human behavior. Information theory is based on the principle that information is measurable and that the rate of innovation is a function of the quantity and variety of information available to a system. Information transmission is the core of this discipline; and, in many ways, items of material culture are a part of and reflect this system. The process of receiving and of using information is the process of our adjusting to the contingencies of the outer environment and of our living effectively within that environment (Wiener 1954).

Game theory is applied to situations in which two individuals, whose interests are not coincident, are in control of different sets of choices. They each endeavor to make their choices in such a manner as to emerge with an advantage, or at least with maximum satisfaction (Rapoport 1959). Examples would be the location of a community, selection of areas to hunt, or the range of natural resources to utilize.

Both game and decision theory can be utilized in formulating models about prehistoric cultural behavior. The basic assumptions of game theory or decision theory are complete rationality and complete knowledge of a situation. The questionable truth of both these assumptions makes this less useful as a descriptive tool than as a model builder.

The systems theory approach for archeologists should involve the creation of models of cultural systems and the expression of these models in directed graphs. The relationships between components of the system should be either logically deduced, or inferred from data already at hand. The various inputs and outputs of the system should be studied and related. Because it is not usually possible to analyze the entire structure of a system, it is necessary to sample it. By creating an explicit expression of the interconnections of the system and the relevant aspects of its environment, we should be able to calculate its behavior in terms of the hypothesized relationships. This is the first test of the reliability of the model.

It is then necessary to attempt to determine the relative magnitudes of as many of the relationships as possible and to determine if these values change as a function of other variables in the system. Critical values or thresholds should be determined for the behavior of the various components and relations in the system.

Proper use of the systems approach will enable archeology to deal with problems of increasingly greater interest and relevance to culture process.

. . . only the modern systems approach promises to get at the full complexity of the interacting phenomena—to see not only the *causes* acting on the phenomena under study, the possible *consequences* of the phenomena, and the possible *mutual interactions* of some of these factors, but also to see the total emergent processes as a function of possible positive and/or negative *feedbacks* mediated by the *selective decisions,* or "choices," of the individuals and groups directly or indirectly involved (Buckley 1967: 80).

𐄁𐄁𐄁𐄁𐄁𐄁𐄁𐄁𐄁𐄁𐄁𐄁𐄁𐄁𐄁𐄁𐄁𐄁𐄁𐄁𐄁𐄁𐄁𐄁𐄁𐄁𐄁𐄁𐄁𐄁𐄁𐄁𐄁

CHAPTER FOUR

THE ECOLOGICAL VIEW OF CULTURE

THE ECOLOGICAL VIEW of culture is among the most productive of systemic frameworks in archeology and anthropology. Ecology is defined as the science of the interrelations between living organisms and their environment or the study of the structure and function of nature (Odum 1953: 3; 1963: 3). Man is a part of this natural system; his relations to other organisms and to his physical surroundings has come to be known as human ecology (Bates 1953). The interaction of most organisms with their environment is closely determined by their biologic needs and their genetic composition.

Man has developed culture, which in various forms acts as a mediator between him and his surroundings. Leslie A. White recognizes this when he defines culture as man's extra-somatic means of adaptation (1959: 8). Some archeologists adopt this view and consider cultural ecology the study of the unfixed, culturally dependent relationships between a human group and its physical surroundings. June Helm sees this view of ecology as stressing "the adaptive and exploitative relations, through the agency of technology, of the human group to its habitat, and the demographic and sociocultural consequences of those relations" (1962: 630).

There are two main ways of relating cultural behavior to environmental situations: "either showing that items of cultural behavior function as part of systems that also include environmental phenomena or else showing that the environmental phenomena are responsible in some manner for the origin or development of the cultural behavior under investigation" (Vayda 1969: *xi*). This means that relationships between the cultural and natural realms are either functional or causal.

As Marston Bates points out, it is probably more useful to "regard ecology as a pervasive point of view rather than as a special subject matter" (1953: 701). Utilizing this perspective one views culture against an environmental background and emphasizes the systemic nature of man's relations to his surroundings. The effect this has on archeology, like that of systems theory, is to shift major research efforts away from an emphasis on entities and toward a concern with relations. The artifact is no longer seen solely as an object with importance of its own, but as a mediator between man and his surroundings. The various cultural subsystems—economic, political, religious—are seen in relation to each other and to the biophysical environment. This is a very practical approach for archeologists in that it embodies several categories of independent data on topography, flora, fauna, and natural resources used that are reasonably easy to infer from the archeological record. Consequently an ecological approach yields many testable hypotheses concerning prehistoric cultural systems.

THE DEVELOPMENT OF THE ECOLOGICAL VIEW

The emphasis on ecology and environmental variables is not an innovation of new archeology. Interest in paleo-environments and food sources goes back almost as far as archeology itself. An early major integrated effort to utilize natural scientists on an archeological expedition was organized by Robert J. Braidwood in 1954–1955. His Iraq-Jarmo project was conceived of, not as a simple site excavation, but as an attack on the ecological problem of the origins of plant and animal domestication (Braidwood and Howe 1960). A geologist, botanist, zoologist, and ceramic technologist were employed to study and analyze their subsystems within the general ecological framework. Remains of early forms of domesticated plants and animals were discovered, and attempts were made at paleo-environmental reconstructions.

This interdisciplinary approach was successful in producing a great deal of natural historical data and in stimulating sufficient interest in these problems and approaches to establish the interdisciplinary expedition as the norm for archeological research. The major objectives of such a project are to collect data concerning the prehistoric flora and fauna, climate, and distribution of archeological sites. For example, Richard S. MacNeish has successfully utilized this type of approach to investigate the problem of early plant domestication in the New World. During several seasons of work in the Tehuacán Valley, Mexico, MacNeish's team found evidence of a series of successively more developed, early domestic plant species including maize (1964 and 1967). From this type of data and a number of excavated sites, he was able to describe the culture-historical sequence of adaptations and settlement for that valley during nine millennia.

Expeditions like these laid the groundwork for the current ecological approach to archeological interpretation by demonstrating the productive results of close cooperation with natural scientists, and the value of their data for a better understanding of the prehistoric record. Their research effort was directed toward a discovery and description of entities, whether they be animals, plants, or climates. This data is very much in line with the traditional goal of describing prehistoric lifeways and establishing a time-space systematics outline for world prehistory.

ECOLOGY AS AN ORGANIZING PRINCIPLE

The ecological approach can be adopted by archeologists not only as a guide to data collection but also as an interpretive framework for viewing culture. Culture is seen as part of a broad system in close interdependence with man's biophysical environment. Artifacts and social organization are no longer seen as entities in themselves, but are viewed in relation to one another and to the general ecosystem of man and nature. The importance of this ecological frame of reference is that, like systems theory itself, it shifts the major interpretive efforts from a concern with entities to an emphasis on relations. This type of approach is suited to the testing of hypotheses and the concern with process.

The ecological view is a refinement and a sophistication of a classic framework for interpreting man's relations with the environment. This view is environmental determinism. That the environment is in some sense determinative of culture and sets the boundaries of human existence is patently obvious (Cannon 1939), but there is also obviously a wide variety of ways of life that are equally possible within the range of temperature, air pressure, and so on, that man can survive. Likewise there is a wide variety of cultures, each of which is consistent with any given environment. Earlier proponents of the view, such as Huntington (1945) and his disciples, sometimes stated the view in the form of laws, asserting that in an environmental situation of a given type, a given culture will be found. This rigid formulation with its lack of allowance for the complex nature of environments and the interaction of cultures with their surroundings has been disconfirmed by the facts of anthropology and archeology. In the broad sense that man and culture are limited by environmental factors, the thesis is obviously true, but not usually productive of detailed hypotheses.

A variation of this view is that of "possibilism." The environment sets limits that provide opportunities for the culture, but does not directly determine details of the culture. Inherent in this view is the idea that culture and environment can be considered as two relatively independent spheres, so that culture can, within very broad limits, develop independently. Such a framework does not provide environmentally deterministic explanations of culture except that the environmental factors do set absolute limits. Within the limits any possible line could be taken, and it is apparent, for example, that mountain peoples are prevented by the environment from developing a tradition of surf riding, while oceanic peoples are strongly (though not necessarily) pressed by the environment to make sea food a dietary staple. Because of the wide variety of cultural possibilities within even such rigid limits as those imposed, for instance, by polar or desert environments, possibilism is accepted as true, but as too general to provide hypotheses and explanations concerning the detail of cultural development.

The ecological approach is a more sophisticated version of environmental determinism. It stresses the interpenetration and interdependence of culture and environment. The complexity of the environmental situations and the detail of man's diverse adaptations to them are emphasized, together with the dynamic aspect of subsistence and other adaptive systems. The ecological approach has made viable and scientifically productive the old insight that the environment is determinative of man's ways.

The approach of Julian H. Steward (1955) has strongly influenced current work. Steward studies cultures through their adaptation to the environment. He generates a taxonomic scheme comprising various levels of socio-cultural complexity that incorporate the observed variability in subsistence techniques and social organization of numerous societies. Steward emphasizes the importance of the "culture core," and seeks cross-cultural regularities in behavior patterns.

An ecologically oriented seminar on the functional classification of cultures produced a seemingly useful framework for archeologists (Beardsley et al. 1956). The proposition is put forth that all human societies can be divided into reasonably homogeneous groups according to their degree of sedentariness. The latter is thought to be related directly to the cultural complexity of the group, or of the surrounding environment. The simplicity and rigidity of this evolutionary framework is closely related to the view of rigid environmental determinism and is thus relatively inadequate as an explanatory model. Hence, it has not gained wide acceptance.

Walter Goldschmidt (1959) presents a view of man in interaction with the environment. His later book *Comparative Functionalism* (1966) provides an operative structure for this approach.

A view of human behavior from a comprehensive, ecological perspective is R. and P. Watson (1969). Here the emphasis is on the elementary logical structures of man's relationships with the physical environment from his origin as a protohuman primate through simple to complex human cultures. These patterns are synthesized from a consideration of the crucial technological and economic relationships between the protohuman, or human, group and the relevant aspects of the environment. The book provides several testable models for the orientation of anthropological and archeological research.

The ecological approach has also stimulated new ideas about how research should be viewed. Anthropologist Edmond R. Leach was one of the first to question the traditional single community-single society approach of field workers (1954). Ethnologists or archeologists investigating an individual settlement cannot attain a complete picture of the ongoing processes (see discussion of the normative approach earlier in this chapter). To do this one must study the total system of interacting communities and their environmental milieu. Leach asserts that the community should be abandoned as the "convenient unit of study" and a broader approach utilized.

Leach's recommendations have been accepted by many archeologists who emphasize the regional approach to archeological survey and site excavation (for example, Struever 1968b and Binford 1964). ". . . the methodology most appropriate for the task of isolating and studying processes of cultural change and evolution is one which is regional in scope . . ." (L. Binford 1964: 425).

With the increasing acceptance of the regional approach and concern for relations with the environment, archeologists have also adopted a number of useful concepts from the biological sciences. Some of them explicitly follow Fredrik Barth's lead in utilizing the notion of the "ecological niche" of a community.

Thus the "environment" of any one ethnic group is not only defined by natural conditions, but also by the presence and activities of the other ethnic groups on which it depends. Each group exploits only a section of the total environment, and leaves large parts of it open for other groups to exploit . . . utilizing some of the concepts of animal ecology, particularly the concept of a *niche*—the place of a group in the total environment, its relations to resources and competitors (Barth 1956: 1079).

This concept is a highly productive way of viewing the cultural system and its environment. The biophysical environment is conceived as one grand system, with cultures participating in different aspects of it and relating to each other and to their surroundings in a variety of ways.

Ecological niches must not be confused with environmental zones and the simple geographic location of settlements. Environmental zones delimit the different regions that are occupied by their own array of plants and animals and are characterized by a particular topographic, climatic, and soil situation.

The ecological niche in which a society participates is not a portion of a geographic region, but is a position within a complex of relationships. The ecological niche is limited by the environmental zones available, each with its characteristic resources, but is more dependent upon the specific range of those resources that the society chooses to utilize. Thus, niches are selectively occupied by a culture and involve the procurement systems of those people, plus their other relations with plants, animals, and human neighbors. Accordingly, two cultures can exist side by side in the same environmental zone or habitat, and participate in quite different ecological niches. A widespread example of this is the sedentary farmer and semisedentary pastoralist whose herds feed on the stubble in farmers' fields and the unoccupied tracts of land in the vicinity (Barth 1961).

The manner in which one views the environment is of great importance. If one is contrasting different regions of a continent or even different continents, it is probable that vast regions will be treated as if they were homogenous. This "coarse-grained" view of the environment can be very useful when investigating certain types of large-scale problems that involve the general workings of cultural systems integrated over entire regions. However, though the coarse-grained view is a highly productive framework for some problems, it obscures too much diversity and variety to be of use for other, smaller-scale problems.

Michael D. Coe and Kent V. Flannery use the term "microenvironment" to refer to a "fine-grained" view of the environment. They considered the use of a macroenvironmental framework inadequate to produce an explanation of early food production in Mesoamerica (1964: 650). They suggest attention should be focused on the behavior of these people in smaller subdivisions of the major ecological zones. They believe that the researcher should analyze the modern-day microecology of the archeological region, especially the seasonal cycles of the wild food sources (1964: 651). Utilizing this method they came to the conclusion:

. . . the basic difference between peoples who subsist on wild foods and those who dwell in permanent villages is that the former must ex-

ploit a wide variety of small ecological niches in a seasonal pattern—
niches which are usually scattered over a wide range of territory—
while the latter may, because of an effective food production,
concentrate on one or on only a few microenvironments which lie relatively close at hand (1964: 654).[1]

Coe and Flannery's emphasis on subsistence as a series of
discrete activities carried out in different localities is central to an
understanding of the transition to sedentary life. In a later publication they extend this type of analysis to a comparison of the
early social organization of the Tehuacán Valley and the Guate-
malan coast (Flannery and Coe 1968). By examining the settlement patterns during the periods of interest and juxtaposing this
data against the distribution of microenvironmental zones and the
resources utilized, the authors are able to determine the relative
degree of subsistence interdependence of the groups studied.

Two useful concepts introduced in this article involve the location of settlements versus the zones utilized by the inhabitants.
A "contagious" distribution refers to a situation where all the settlements are in one zone and all utilize the surrounding zones in a
similar way. A "symbiotic" pattern is one in which settlements are
spread over the different microenvironmental zones with trade and
interaction among them.

Coe and Flannery's earlier emphasis on microenvironments
has been partially replaced by a concern with the procurement
systems of subsistence resources. Flannery has argued:

. . . it appears that sometimes a group's basic "adaptation" may not
even be to the "microenvironments" within a zone, but rather to a
small series of plant and animal genera whose ranges cross-cut several
environments (1968: 67).

[1] It should be noted that the words "ecological niche" and "environmental
zone" are not clearly differentiated in this passage, as is often the case in
archeological and anthropological writing. As already pointed out, a zone or
habitat is a geographic location, while the term "ecological niche" should
be used to mean a position in a system of relations. Potential niches may
closely parallel the environmental zones, but they are not synonymous.

This approach more closely approximates the concept of ecological niche and reflects a greater interest in the actual activities and resources prehistoric men were utilizing than in the habitats from which these resources come (see pp. 94–95 of this chapter).

TRADE, BOUNDARIES, AND INTERACTION SPHERES

Acceptance by archeologists of the ecological view of culture has caused a re-evaluation of many traditional models of cultural activity. The models that a researcher utilizes will influence the types of inferences he makes and the directions his investigations will follow. Those who use the ecological approach emphasize the importance of considering culture as a system with many subsystems and are deeply concerned with the relational aspects of these interacting systems.

Major reorientations become necessary with considerable attention being given to subjects such as exchange, trade, and more general forms of interaction. This is exemplified in Colin Renfrew's article "Trade and Culture Process in European Prehistory" (Renfrew 1969). He criticizes the widespread use of diffusion and invasion as the primary means of explanation of culture change. He advocates the "quantitative study of economic systems, and especially trading systems, for an understanding of the culture process at work" (1969: 160). Instead of looking to outside influence as the causal factor, one must closely examine the internal workings of the cultural community and its constituent subsystems. Renfrew's interest centers on trade in prehistoric Europe. He asserts that the economic importance of trade has been misinterpreted in several ways (1969: 151). Rather than looking for ways that "outside civilizations" impose new culture forms, the archeologist should be concerned with the functional role trade and interaction play in the cultural system. Trade could encourage a change in community patterning or social organization in order to handle goods more efficiently, or it can be a source of innovative ideas.

Examples of long-distance trade and its effects are found in a variety of prehistoric societies and may play a central role in cultural development. Howard Winters suggests, basing himself upon data from various sites and burials in the midwestern United States, that "marine shell and copper were being distributed over vast distances within eastern North America by the third millennium B.C." There is also good evidence that the later vast trade network that links the various regional traditions of the Hopewellian Interaction Sphere is rooted in the simpler exchange systems of this earlier period (Winters 1968: 219).

An example of a trading system that is receiving increased attention from archeologists is the early prehistoric obsidian trade in the Near East (G. Wright 1969). By means of trace-element analysis it is possible to pinpoint the location of the source of a piece of obsidian. The sources of this volcanic glass that was used for tools and ornaments are very limited and exist predominantly in Anatolia. As early as the seventh millennium B.C. there is evidence for trade in obsidian as far away as southern Palestine (Jericho) and southwestern Iran (Deh Luran). Trade in commonly recognized status symbols may serve as a mechanism linking high ranking lineages from various regions. Gary Wright considers the primary importance of the long-distance trade network in the Near East to be "the movement of domesticated wheat from the Jordan Valley into the Zagros-Taurus arc and sheep from the latter region into the Levant" (G. Wright 1969: 81). Thus, Wright asserts, the obsidian trade in this instance was "an agent in communication"—it had a cultural significance which far exceeded the economic value of the obsidian (1969: 78).

Traditionally, archeologists were often interested in trade and interaction, but their research involved only the formulation of distribution maps for certain kinds of raw materials and artifacts, rather than a discussion of the mechanics and effects of the exchanges themselves. "To assert that trade occurred answers nothing. One must attempt to demonstrate how the system operated, what its consequences were, and the hypotheses must be testable" (G. Wright 1969: 84).

The interest in trade systems is paralleled by a reconsideration of many other traditional subjects by archeologists, and by ecologically oriented anthropologists as well. Included in these are questions of the nature and role of nomadism, the function of boundaries or frontiers, and the meaning of culture areas.

Traditional ideas concerning nomads and pastoralists have been revised to reflect their central role in trading networks and their complex interactions with more settled communities. Owen Lattimore's treatment of frontier populations in central Asia has been crucial in this re-evaluation. Lattimore castigates the old idea of "waves of nomads beating against the shores of sedentarism and civilization" (1962). Closer examination of the actual evidence indicates that the simplistic picture painted by the ancient historians is far from the real situation. Instead of a distinct difference between settled and nomadic people along a distinct border, one should conceive of a continuum of degrees of sedentarism from the city centers to the marginal part-time farmers, and out to the full-time pastoralist nomads. A small shift at either end of the continuum can cause a shift all along the spectrum of different settlement types. Thus the Mongolians themselves would not have been powerful enough to defeat the Chinese empire, except that their unsettling influence along the margins of the empire persuaded many marginal farmers to give up their sedentary ways and created an imbalance in the whole civilizational network. This model can be profitably applied to urban instability in Mesopotamian and Mexican history.

The importance of frontiers and boundaries in culture process has been recognized by several archeologists (for example, L. Binford 1968b and Flannery 1965). We may define the difference between these two concepts as follows: A frontier involves processes of integration of new areas into older (more developed) traditions, whereas the function of boundaries is to separate regions along physical or conceptual lines.

The current ideas on frontiers go back to Carl Sauer (1930, 1963), who conceived of the successive frontiers of American settlement as a "series of secondary culture hearths." Because of the demographic and physical situation of these regions, innovation was stimulated. Boundaries between ecological zones are areas with the greatest diversity of living species and as such they offer unique opportunities for food collectors. By bringing some of the plant species across the boundaries into different environmental zones, the direction of natural selection is changed. Some investigators believe this to be an important factor in the development of agriculture (Braidwood 1960, L. Binford 1968b, and G. Wright 1969).

A transitional ecological situation, as described above, is known as an ecotone. The ecotone will contain a greater diversity of species than either of the zones it borders, and hence is a rich area to exploit for food.

A. L. Kroeber divided the North American continent into a series of culture areas according to the societies that had inhabited them in the ethnographic past (1939). Binford has suggested that this approach be modified, and has constructed a tripartite scheme based on a concept introduced by J. R. Caldwell (1964), the "interaction sphere." Binford's scheme emphasizes the multivariate nature of culture and the need to analyze cultural phenomena in a systemic framework. His first category is the "tradition," which is a reflection of stylistic variability in artifacts (L. Binford 1965: 208). The second category is that of the "interaction sphere," and is defined in terms of widely exchanged goods that occur in a context of social distinctiveness. The third category is characterized by artifacts used primarily for coping directly with the physical environment, and is called an "adaptive area." By considering geographic divisions according to these three different categories, it is possible for archeologists to incorporate a multidimensional approach into cultural interpretations.

SETTLEMENT PATTERNS

Another type of archeological research that has received considerable impetus from adoption of the ecological approach is prehistoric settlement-pattern studies. Early studies of the distribution of archeological sites had been made by Braidwood (1937) and Willey (1953), but the approach came into its own with the publication of *Prehistoric Settlement Patterns in the New World* (Willey 1956). In the introduction to this work Willey says that:

In settlement, man inscribes upon the landscape certain modes of his existence. These settlement arrangements relate to the adjustments of man and culture to environment and to the organization of society in the broadest sense (1956: 1).

This concern with configurations of sites was innovative, but a restricted view of the data is suggested when Willey says: "Viewed archeologically, settlement patterns are, like any prehistoric residue, the incomplete and fragmentary oddments of something that was once vital and whole" (1956: 1).

Some archeologists have a more positivistic view and utilize archeological settlement patterns as a valuable source of data for testing hypotheses on a wide range of topics. These successive configurations of communities can yield inferences that are relevant to various topics concerning population, subsistence, sociopolitical systems, trade, and warfare.

A valuable source of techniques is the work of human geographers in coping with distributional data. These researchers are concerned with similar problems of description, comparison, and process, and work with data in many ways similar to that of archeology, but from the present and historical periods. The forms of settlement data archeologists deal with are density, agglomeration, scatter, extent, orientation, shape, and topographic location of prehistoric communities. Three types of frameworks are available for investigations of the settlement data. The first is a diachronic or processual framework, where one variable is studied in one region over time. The second approach is a synchronic or functional one, where several variables are examined in one region at one time interval. The final framework is the comparative one in which one views a single variable in several regions.

Numerous settlement-pattern models utilized by geographers could be productive if applied to archeological data. One of these models, "principle of least-cost," has been used in a limited form to investigate settlement patterns in the southwest United States (Fritz and Plog 1970). Their basic assumption is that settlements will be located in such a way as to minimize the effort expended in dealing with the environment. Thus, necessities such as water, fuel, and agricultural land could be the prime determinants of site location. By recording the varying distances to these resources during successive periods in a region, information is gained concerning the relative importance of these factors in settlement location in the respective periods.

A method developed by plant ecologists Clark and Evans (1954) may be used to help describe the nature of site distributions in a region. By measuring the distance to the nearest neighboring community for each site, it is possible to calculate an index of clustering for the distribution (Plog 1968, Adams and Nissen in press).

Another method that can be used to describe site distributions is to cover the region with a rectangular grid and then count the number of sites within each grid square. If the sites are randomly distributed throughout the region, the patterning of sites per grid square will approximate what is known as a "Poisson distribution," a mathematical representation that approximates a random distribution. The divergence of the observed from the expected values will give a quantitative measure of the clustering or nonclustering (even dispersal) distribution of these communities (King 1969).

A very important geographic model formulated by Christaller and refined by Lösch is known as central place theory (Haggett 1965, Berry 1967, and King 1969). The basic assumption is that successively larger communities will provide larger numbers of services for the surrounding smaller communities. Farming settlements on an agriculturally homogeneous plain can best utilize the land if they are arranged in a hexagonal lattice distribution. The most efficient location of larger settlements would be in the center of these hexagons of six villages, with each large settlement serving six surrounding villages (see Figure IV-1). Thus it is possible to construct the theoretical optimum distribution of villages and towns in a region if the critical variables for site location are given, and if one can assume certain uniformities in the physical situation. Prehistoric settlement patterns can be compared to the derived models, and organizing principles can be inferred from the results of the comparison. The deviations of the observed patterns will also yield valuable data on settlement interaction.

Another method of comparing a particular observed set of data to expected values over a region is known as trend-surface

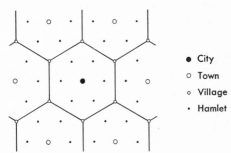

Figure IV-1: Ideal Distribution of Settlements
According to Christaller's Theory
of Hexagonal Arrangements

analysis, or computer simulation analysis, and has not yet been attempted in archeology, although this type of method has great potential. The expected values of the phenomenon are put in explicit form (often an equation) and mathematically compared with the empirical situation. Best fits of proposed hypotheses can then be objectively determined and residual values can lead to further refinement of the proposed model (Haggett 1965, King 1969, Doran 1970, Cole and King 1968).

Applications of the methods of locational analysis have not yet been widely published in archeological literature, but several archeologists have presented papers describing the use of them, and the trend is toward increasing utilization of these techniques and models (Plog 1968, Struever 1969b, H. Wright 1969, Redman and P. Watson 1970).

AN APPLICATION OF THE ECOLOGICAL APPROACH:
THE FOOD-PRODUCING TRANSFORMATION

The ecological approach has been productively applied to various problems of general archeological interest. One of the most important and much discussed subjects of inquiry is the origins and early development of plant and animal domestication in Southwest Asia. V. Gordon Childe termed this crucial transformation the "Agricultural Revolution" and proposed that the central causal factor was the increasing desiccation of the environment which resulted in plants, animals, and men being brought into close proximity and interdependence by the shrinking oases (1937 and 1942). This hypothesis lost most of its support as information accumulated on paleoclimates and early site locations. Robert J. Braidwood then proposed a broader explanation based on the concept of a nuclear zone where potential domesticates existed for a long period of time. Increasing familiarization with these resources ultimately led to their utilization and domestication.

Recently, other hypotheses have been put forth to explain this process (L. Binford 1968b; Flannery 1965, 1969). Binford assesses the inadequacy of the past explanations of the origins of agriculture and proposes one that is based on ecological and demographic variables. He asserts (with reference to population biologists) that successfully adapted hunting and gathering communities will homeostatically maintain their population below the carrying capacity of the land either by limiting their population growth by means of cultural regulation, or by emigration from the parent community. This second method, or budding off, is suggested as an important stimulus to the occupation of new and marginal lands. Binford suggests that these people with subsistence patterns well adapted to their local environments would change their way of life only if their current situation underwent some important disturbance. He cites such possible disturbances: a change in the physical environment that would reduce the food sources available, or an increase in the population density until it reaches the carrying capacity of the land. Binford points to the lack of convincing data to support a climatic change (but see recent paper by H. E. Wright 1968) and suggests that the explanation of the origin of agriculture can be found in demographic pressures that forced settlements into areas marginal to the gathering type of existence.

Flannery builds on the Binford model of demographic pressures on the margins of optimal zones. He suggests that a critical factor antecedent to the agricultural revolution was the adoption of a "broad spectrum" resource utilization by upper Paleolithic peoples (Flannery 1969). This subsistence pattern allowed a more sedentary existence and encouraged the development of several cultural manifestations that facilitated domestication. Flannery cites Harlan and Zohary (1966) when he proposes that the hunting and gathering adaptation would be too successful in the centers of the optimal zones to stimulate a transition. He, like Binford, points to the marginal areas as the likely centers of

innovation. He suggests that the development of animal domestication was an effort to "bank" against poor agricultural seasons.
Both Flannery and Binford offer stimulating hypotheses, but these
are only a beginning. They do encompass the great diversity of information available, but the available data are inadequate for testing the various aspects of these explanations.

Several major expeditions in Southwest Asia have concentrated on lessening this problem of insufficient data for testing.
The two publications which have contributed the most information
on this subject, Braidwood and Howe (1960), and Hole, Flannery,
and Neely (1969), have employed ecology as their organizing
principle.

SUMMARY

In this section we have considered the concept of culture, as it has
been conceived in the past and as it might be most usefully conceived in the future. We have been primarily interested in attempts to understand or explain culture and culture process. Archeologists who operate with an explicitly scientific orientation,
like all scientists, must hold that their subject matter is empirically
observable and hence potentially knowable. Therefore, scientific
archeologists assume that the relevant aspects of prehistoric cultures must be observable in the archeological record. In accord-
ance with this necessary operating assumption, scientifically oriented archeologists utilize a view of culture which stresses the
observable behavioral aspects of the societies in question, rather
than the unobservable shared ideas and norms.

They assert that a systemic view of culture is a realistic and
productive framework for archeological interpretations. The major
emphasis is on relations among entities, rather than on the entities
themselves. This concern with relations facilitates the formulation
of explanations and the study of process.

Another discipline which promises to aid the incorporation of a systemic view of culture into archeological analysis is general systems theory itself. Systems theorists are building a corpus of laws and methods to help investigate systems of all types. The utilization of this approach enables archeologists to construct more realistic and testable models of human behavior, and it can play a key role in determining relevant categories of data and necessary avenues of investigation.

The ecological view of culture has already achieved widespread acceptance among archeologists and is more readily applicable to archeological data than the more general systems theory. An ecological approach emphasizes the importance of elements of the biophysical environment—plants, animals, climate, and topography—but its real contribution is the perspective it gives to research. Through it, the investigator views man and nature as participating in a series of dynamic and interacting systems. This concept of interpenetration of culture and environment leads to productive and testable models.

In Chapters 1 and 2 we outline and discuss the theoretical requirements of archeology as an explicitly scientific discipline. In Chapter 3 and the present chapter we are concerned with the central interpretive concept of archeological analysis: culture, and with possible explanatory frameworks to use in studying it. In Chapter 5 we treat a series of methods and techniques that are appropriate to an explicitly scientific archeology, and that will help operationalize the theoretical frameworks and perspectives we discuss in the previous chapters.

Part Three

Incorporating the Logic of Science Into Archeological Method

゠゠

CHAPTER FIVE

METHODS AND THE
ARCHEOLOGICAL RECORD

SO FAR WE HAVE CONSIDERED, for the most part, rather broad, theoretical subjects: epistemological issues concerned with the logic of science and the nature of culture. In this chapter we will turn to some very specific topics and indicate what is entailed methodologically if archeologists assume the theoretical position discussed in the preceding chapters. The first consideration is the nature of the archeological record.

NATURE OF THE ARCHEOLOGICAL RECORD

The traditional approach to the archeological record usually stresses the limits of the information available to the archeologist because of lack of preservation.

What we have at our disposal, as prehistorians, is the accidentally surviving durable remnants of material culture, which we interpret as best we may, and inevitably the peculiar quality of this evidence dictates the sort of information we can obtain from it (Piggott 1965: 5).

Proponents of the new approach concentrate on the positive aspects of the archeological record by emphasizing the systematic

order of the surviving remains. This order is related to prehistoric
activities and events in ways that the archeologist can ascertain.
Thus, he can obtain from the archeological record information on
many aspects of an extinct cultural system (see earlier discussion,
Chapter 2 here, and Hill 1970b):

It has often been suggested that we cannot dig up a social system or
ideology. Granted we cannot excavate a kinship terminology or a philosophy, but we can and do excavate the material items which functioned together with these more behavioral elements within the appropriate cultural subsystems. The formal structure of artifact assemblages
together with the between element contextual relationships should and
do present a systemic and understandable picture of *the total extinct*
cultural system (L. Binford 1962: 218–19).

In other words, theoretically speaking, the materials in the
ground and their spatial distributions represent the total behavior
patterns of the ancient culture. Practically speaking, however,
these are certainly variations in the nature and amount of data at
some times and places; for example, at some one site there may
not be enough data to permit independent tests of certain hypotheses and therefore they must remain unconfirmed. The problem of negative evidence also frequently arises. Because an element or complex is not directly observable does not mean that it
did not exist in the living culture nor does it mean that we cannot
infer its presence some other way. If, in the course of investigation
of some particular problem, negative evidence becomes pertinent
to the testing of a hypothesis, our first assumption should be that
the situation can be positively attacked. For instance, it has often
been noted that bone tools are abundant and varied in the Upper
Paleolithic industries of Europe whereas in the preceding Mousterian bone tools are virtually absent. Traditionally it was claimed
that there is a major break between these two manifestations. If it
could be established that the lack of bone in Mousterian industries
is a real lack and not just the result of differential preservation,
then this would help confirm the major break hypothesis. On the

other hand, if it could be established that the lack of bone is owing to differential preservation, then the hypothesis would be disconfirmed.

One might choose not to use the bone data (or lack of it) in testing his hypothesis because of the potential difficulties of working with negative evidence. He might instead approach the situation positively by seeking some means of inferring information about bone as it might be reflected in other preserved items, for example, by distinctive wear on stone tools used to work bone.

The logical position of archeology with respect to the limitations of the archeological record should be a strongly positivistic one: The information is there, it is the investigator's task to devise means to extract it.

The practical limitations on our knowledge of the past are not inherent in the nature of the archeological record; the limitations lie in our methodological naiveté, in our lack of development [of] principles determining the relevance of archeological remains to propositions regarding processes and events of the past (Binford 1968a: 23).

That is, there *are always* relations between the debris and the actions of ancient peoples and the events and social structures of ancient societies. The archeologist is sometimes limited in his ability to discover just what these relations are. Once he does work them out, however, his only other limitation is the extent of his ability to discern the significance of the reconstructed objects and events. Even in the absence of postaboriginal disturbance, to formulate hypotheses and test implications concerning the prehistoric social organization and to articulate these with the actual debris recovered from the ground requires great care and ingenuity.

Having said this, we can also recognize the truth in the claim that sometimes we do not have enough data to make any of these multilevel inferences. Some information may be lost before the site is ever investigated because of such phenomena as slope wash, weathering of exposed items, and disturbance by animals and humans. But—except in cases of serious postoccupational disturbance—limitations are imposed by our own abilities. The relation between the debris and the original objects (and even between the absence of the debris and the original objects) and the relations between the original objects and social structure are there. It is only up to us to find methods of discovering them and interpreting them. There are practical limitations, but concentrated attacks are showing that archeologists can go further than has been thought possible during most of the previous history of the endeavor.

RELEVANT DATA

Relevant archeological data consist of anything observable which pertains to the solving of the investigator's particular problem. In order to determine which data to collect, the investigator must formulate hypotheses and deduce test implications from them. Relevant data are then those data necessary to check the implications and may include anything observable at the archeological site, as well as information obtained elsewhere (see p. 116). Relevant data may include not only architecture and artifacts but also the condition of the artifacts, whether they are charred, broken, or worn, as well as data that are not strictly artifactual, such as pollen, splinters of animal bone from ancient garbage dumps, bits of carbonized plant remains, or impressions of plant remains in mud walls and floors, the chemical constituents of various strata at a site, and so on. The spatial distributions and associations of objects in the site may be especially relevant.

Only data considered to be relevant will be collected. One seldom collects what one is not looking for. For example, before the development of the radiocarbon dating technique in the late 1940's, little or no attention was paid to bits of charcoal in archeological excavations. After 1948, however, such bits of charcoal were eagerly sought and carefully collected for submission to laboratories equipped to assay their C–14 content. Also, before the tiny stone tools called "microliths" were known to exist in open sites in Southwest Asia, hundreds of them were shoveled out of excavations without being noticed. After attention had been called to them, excavators found them in quantities.

While it might be assumed that these examples are rare or unusual cases, the same problem occurs at every excavation. One cannot possibly hope to record every bit of minutiae of nonartifactual information or even to be sure that every "artifact" is properly perceived as such. One must obviously generalize at some level, and the level chosen is that appropriate to the problem at hand. If one takes the narrow inductivist position (p. 10 of Chapter 1) of allowing the data to speak for themselves, one is really listening to only a small part of the potential data.

Because it is literally impossible to record everything, it is necessary to emphasize careful research design and clear formulation of questions, together with specification of the kinds of data necessary to answer them. One must decide what to recover on the basis of formulated questions, not simply on the basis of an intuitive concept of the nature of data. Data are then sought in full recognition of the fact that certain other data undoubtedly will be partly or wholly neglected.

It should be made clear, however, that the extremes of both positions just described—recording all the data and recording only the relevant data—are impossible to achieve. Because it is impossible for an investigator to determine beforehand exactly how much and what kind of data is relevant, he always records more than appears necessary to answer most questions. It is also true that by use of some ingenuity and sophistication, he can wring quantities of information from relatively minor data items. For instance, a single fish scale may be sufficient to inform us of the season when the fish was caught and the ecological essentials of the stream or other body of water from which it came.

The method advocated is simply explicit application of procedures used in any scientific discipline. First, the archeological investigator should decide exactly what question he is asking, and next, what kinds of information will answer his question. It should be noted that the question must be a specific one. To express one's interest in broad, general areas such as "urbanization" is not sufficient; these interests or topics must be approached through specific hypotheses to be tested. Third, the investigator must devise ways to get the information from the ground. Information, again, can be anything observable that helps answer his questions, and may be quite remote from the traditional categories of "material culture" items. At Star Carr, for instance, a large percentage of the analysis was devoted to nonartifactual material such as cast-off antlers used to determine the season the site was occupied (J. G. D. Clark 1954). The minimum number of individual deer was also calculated, enabling the excavators to estimate the amount of meat available during the period of occupation.

It should be clear that an expanded concept of the nature of archeological data is necessary, and that these data need not necessarily come from the sites themselves. Observations made on ethnographic data, and replicative or imitative experiments can be utilized in testing hypotheses involving uniformitarian principles (see pp. 49–51 above) of archeological interest.

At the sites themselves, archeological data consist of observable artifactual items (bone and stone tools, pottery, and so on), as well as architecture and "nonartifactual" remains (animal bones, carbonized botanical remains or impressions of plant parts, soil chemistry, pollen, and so on), plus the other observable attributes of artifacts (wear patterns, charring, and so on) and spatial relationships of all these. Spatial relationships refer to the three-dimensional distribution of artifactual and nonartifactual material in the ground (where it occurs and how it is lying), that is, the distribution of artifactual and nonartifactual material with respect to architecture and other features including the ground matrix.

This network of interrelationships makes up the structure of

the site (Struever 1969a: 1; Longacre 1968: 91). The spatial relationships delineate the depositional history of the site. It is important not merely to record the stratigraphic levels of a site, but to
excavate the site with respect to these levels. The basic assumption
is that the vertical and horizontal distribution of all material making up an archeological site is as important as the material itself,
because that distribution reflects patterned human cultural activity
just as much as do the form, style, and manufacturing technique of
the artifacts.

This emphasis on spatial relationships implies that we can
delimit *activity areas* by plotting tool types or other artifacts
against precise provenience with respect to ground matrix, architectural features, or each other. (For examples of activity clusters
and activity areas see Hole, Flannery and Neely 1969: Fig. 10;
Hill 1966; De Lumley 1969; J. D. Clark 1969: Pl. 14).

From activity-specific tool kits it is possible to move to questions of social organization and social stratification. For example,
Deetz describes the differential distribution of items made and
used by men as opposed to women among the Chumash Indians:

. . . baskets and milling equipment among the southern California
Chumash of the early nineteenth century, and perhaps even earlier,
are quite uniform over the entire area known to have been occupied
by these people. Such uniformity contrasts sharply with the diversity
seen in such artifacts as arrowheads, which differ considerably from
site to site. The pattern is one of widespread rules for female manufactures, and isolated sets of somewhat different rules for male manufactures. . . . This can only mean that women were 'widespread' and
men 'isolated' (Deetz 1967: 94–95).

Deetz then relates this artifact distribution to the Chumash
custom of patrilocal residence and local exogamy. Such a pattern
would result in the men, and hence their skills and manufactures,
staying in the village whereas the women (and their skills and
manufactures) move out of their native villages and into those of
their husbands. As a result, items made and used by men would

have a discrete distribution with each village characterized by its own style of projectile points, while items made and used by women would be distributed much more widely.

Thus, from the distribution of tool types and clusters which he is able to define as female- and male-specific, Deetz can arrive at conclusions concerning the social organization of the human group that left the remains. Hill and Longacre were also able to identify male- and female-associated items and to use these in their analyses (see pp. 36 and 45 of Chapter 2).

Another important aspect of spatial relationships which has long been a matter for concern among archeologists is the nature and distribution of grave goods. For instance, in Adams' study of social evolution in ancient Sumer, he utilizes as an important line of evidence the amount of luxury goods found in excavated graves.

In the late Ubaid period significant differentiation in grave wealth was almost entirely absent. . . . [But by Early Dynastic times] The impression of differentiation [given by architectural remains] is confirmed and amplified by a study of tomb furniture. One of the clearest indices to wealth is the presence of copper, as well as more precious metals. . . . The previously unparalleled concentrations of metal that appear in a few graves . . . must indicate a correspondingly increased range of differentiation in wealth. And while copper becomes *le metal d'echange par excellence* by the Early Dynastic III period . . . on the whole it remained of so high a value that ordinary craftsmen and even minor bureaucrats were limited to at most a few implements of this material for which they were at pains to keep an accounting. . . . In other words, copper implements and vessels (to say nothing of gold or silver) qualitatively increase the implication of wealth for the burial assemblages in which they occur, as opposed to those in which they are lacking (Adams 1966: 95, 98–99).

Adams then examines known graves of the Early Dynastic period at several sites and finds that:

In sum, insofar as grave goods reflect the general distribution of wealth, there is evidence for a decisive increase in social differentiation in the cities during the course of the Early Dynastic period (Adams 1966: 100).

Another and very recent example of grave goods analysis is described in the paper presented by Longacre at the Thirty-fifth Annual Meeting of the Society for American Archaeology, Mexico City, on May 1, 1970. The paper is titled "Analysis of Burials from the Grasshopper Ruin, Arizona." In it he describes a factor analysis (see pp. 147–50 below for a brief discussion of this statistical technique) which was used to elicit the relationships among grave objects. This statistical technique yielded six factors, or sets, of objects that tended to occur frequently together, and these factors could then be used as units of analysis. He relates the factors (or clusters) to chronological periods, sex, age, and status of individuals.

Activity areas may occur horizontally across a site, and they may occur vertically. Various members of a single culture may perform different activities in different parts of the same site at about the same time. The resulting horizontal distribution of cultural debris and features might indicate or delineate butchering, cooking, sleeping, and toolmaking activity areas, which the archeologist would probably interpret correctly as different activities of the same people. However, it is quite possible that at some sites (Paleolithic rock shelters, for instance, or riverbank shellmounds) activity clusters may accumulate vertically, and that diachronic inferences may be mistakenly drawn from them. For example, members of the same culture may return to the same place several times over a period of a few months or a few years and perform varying functions there (sleeping and cooking one time, butchering another, toolmaking on a third occasion, butchering and cooking on a fourth, and so on). There will result a vertical distribution or cultural stratigraphy which, though actually reflecting only changes in activities or functions within a single culture, might be interpreted as replacements of one culture by another. The possibility of mistakenly interpreting vertical ordering of activity clusters or areas as a diachronic sequence of cultural replacement is especially relevant to studies based on seriation, because the basic as-

sumption of such seriational studies is that sharp changes in artifact types and frequencies indicate cultural breaks or transitions.

In this section so far (pp. 114–20) we have made the
following points:

1) Data to the problem-oriented archeologist are anything observable
   which help him solve his problem.
2) Because only data considered actually or potentially relevant will
   be recorded and/or collected, one should proceed by explicitly defining the problem to be solved or question to be answered, explicitly defining the data needed to solve the problem, and explicitly
   defining the techniques necessary to collect that data.

Because relevant data may be anything observable, a greatly
expanded concept of data results from this kind of emphasis, one
of the most important aspects of which is the general topic of spatial relations or the structure of the site. The importance of contextual relationships of artifacts and architecture was strongly emphasized by Walter W. Taylor (1948) in his discussion of the
conjunctive approach, and, as indicated by the examples in this
chapter and in Chapter 2 (Deetz and Adams, Longacre and Hill),
is indispensable to contemporary problem-oriented archeology. As
this situation indicates, fundamental field method is the area of
greatest continuity between past and present developments in archeology. Walter W. Taylor's conjunctive approach and Sir Mortimer Wheeler's discussions of the importance of natural stratigraphic relationships set standards for all archeologists everywhere.

The area of contrast lies in the strong emphasis of the theoretically oriented archeologists on explicit definition of problem,
of data needed to solve it, and of techniques necessary to collect
the data. This emphasis, plus the rapid increase in available techniques and equipment (resistivity devices and magnetometers, flotation, the multitude of dating processes, and so on), means that,
though basic field methods have remained the same, there is a disjunction between problem and method for attacking it on the one

hand, and the day-to-day pragmatics of actual techniques used and organization of field work on the other. This disjunction is pointed out and discussed by Struever:

. . . if a major purpose of archeology is to elucidate cultural process by *explaining* prehistoric episodes of change or stability, then the strategy of archeology must shift to long-term programs of field work and analysis (Struever 1968a:133).

He discusses in detail his own research program in the lower Illinois Valley to illustrate his basic point that the organization of archeological research no longer reflects accurately what are considered to be the most important research problems, nor is it able to incorporate adequately the multitudinous techniques available to solve them. This difficulty is becoming more and more acute and as yet no satisfactory solution has been developed. Further discussion will be found in Chapter 6 below.

ARCHEOLOGICAL SAMPLING

Once the problem is defined, the next step for the archeologist is to specify the kind of data needed to solve the problem. When this has been done, at least in operational terms, the question of sampling arises. Archeologists sample continuously: Choosing a site to excavate is sampling the universe of excavatable sites. Moreover, sites are very rarely excavated in their entireties—hence what is excavated is a sample of the site. It is important to make this sampling process, at whatever level, explicit and systematic. Sampling should be an integral part of the research design, and several fundamental aspects of it need consideration here.

Sampling is a compromise; it is a means of getting an adequate representation of some universe of data without having to deal with all the data in that universe. It is impossible and unnecessary to recover all the data of any one kind. Sampling is the only solution, but before proceeding with sampling techniques one

must decide how large his sample should be. The decision concerning sample size is based on the nature of the problem being
investigated and on the desired degree of confirmation of hypothetical solutions to it. There is no standard percentage figure that
automatically yields a valid sample size. If a systematic surface
collecuon is to be made of a sample of the 500 grid squares on
some particular site, then a 10% sample would probably be statistically adequate. But if the universe consists, not of 500 grid
squares on a site surface, but of 20 rooms in a prehistoric pueblo,
then a 10% sample is probably not adequate because a sample of
2 is not large enough to deal with statistically. In general, the ability of the sample to approximate the reality of the universe being
sampled increases as the absolute sample size increases. But after
a certain minimum adequate size of sample is reached, a point of
diminishing returns is also quickly reached, so that, for example,
doubling the sample size does not give a characterization twice as
close to the reality of the universe being sampled as does the un-
dc:bled sample. (For more complete and detailed discussions, see
Haggett 1965; Deming 1950; Ragir 1967.)

    Once he has determined how large a sample is needed, the
investigator must decide what kind of sampling procedure to use.
One very important requirement for any scientific sampling procedure is that it avoid human bias. To do this one must employ
some form of probabilistic sampling design. There are two important considerations with respect to this sampling design which
must be assessed from the point of view of the primary goal of the
research project in question: (1) If the goal is to describe the
range of variation within the universe (for example, the site) as
accurately as possible, then the investigator must be careful to use
a sampling technique that will result in a sample representative of
this range of variation. For example, in a study of the relationship
of surface archeological material at two prehistoric sites in Turkey
(Redman and P. Watson 1970), we found the simple random sample of grid squares to be collected at our first site was not satisfac-

tory because it resulted in "blank spots" on the site where no sample squares happened to fall (Fig V-1). This random sample eliminated human bias, but, because our purpose was not simply to sample the total assemblage but to trace the variation in distributional patterns across the site, we found a modified random sample much more satisfactory. For the second site we used such a modified random sample, called a "stratified unaligned systematic sample," which eliminated the disadvantage just discussed of the simple random sample but retained its unbiased nature (Fig. V-2).

In this example, the investigators' primary concern was to obtain representation. But, (2) if the primary goal is statistical description and comparison between samples, the investigator must take this into account to allow for assumptions of a random sample, of a normal distribution, and so on. For instance, if the universe to be sampled is a series of projectile points and the investigator, in attempting to define the average dimensions of the points, measures only the perfect specimens (that is, excludes from his sample all incomplete projectile points), his sample may be badly skewed. The perfect ones may comprise a nonrandom sample because their perfection is controlled by some additional factor (such as nature of the raw material) other than the attributes ostensibly being measured (length, width, and so on).

In the second example the investigator did not give sufficient thought to ensuring the randomness of his sample. As these two examples indicate, there is no simple solution to what sampling procedures are valid for what purposes, but there are many different possibilities (see Berry and Baker 1968; Deming 1950; Haggett 1965; Hill 1966; Ragir 1967; Redman 1971).

In making any decision on sampling procedure, whether it is which site or which area within a site to excavate, pragmatic considerations are important. One must weigh the cost of obtaining a sample against the value of the data recovered. For example, if the portion of the site selected by the sampling procedure for excava-

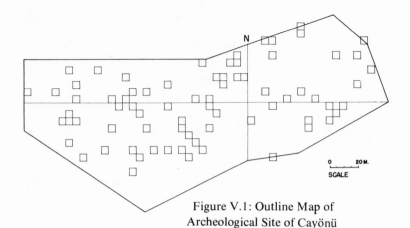

Figure V.1: Outline Map of
Archeological Site of Cayönü

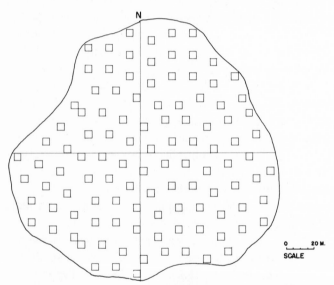

Figure V.2: Outline Map of
Archeological Site of Girikihaciyan

tion is covered by a tree or large boulders, the time and money involved in sampling it may not be worthwhile. Usually some non-
biased means of selecting another sample area is the best solution.
The important point is that pragmatic considerations should not

be the primary determinants of procedure and should not bias the sample.

ANALYTICAL PROCEDURES

Once the sampling process is completed and the data collected, analysis and interpretation begin. How one analyzes and interprets depends on how one digs and records. This means the investigator starts with a question *and* with a clear idea of the probable answer (that is, a hypothesis or set of hypotheses). He then chooses digging and recording methods and techniques based on adequate sampling procedures with these hypotheses in mind. That is, he decides what data are relevant to the testing of the hypotheses and how best to obtain them. But as he excavates and data accumulate and are analyzed, he may alter his hypotheses. When this happens, he will probably also alter his digging and recording and hence his future methods of analysis.

Most excavators follow the general outlines of this procedure —altering excavation techniques as data accumulate—but often there is a long lag between digging (data accumulation), analysis of data, and modification of methods of data accumulation. Ideally, a shortened or abbreviated feedback cycle should be maintained so that analysis keeps pace with field work and the two constantly influence each other. New data are analyzed and the results are used immediately to assess the state of the basic hypothesis or hypotheses. If the latter must be altered, then digging and recording methods must also be altered.

The specific nature and amount of analysis depends on the problem. If it is a culture historical one, then the data sought and the analytical methods used are different from such procedures if one's interest is in general anthropological questions. However, these two goals are not necessarily mutually exclusive nor is one good and the other bad. Purely descriptive studies of housetype distributions, for instance, or of Halaf painted pottery, may be useful to the social scientifically oriented observer if they lay out and classify material so that he can see in what direction lie the questions interesting to him. However, such an observer would not consider "doing" the Halaf pottery, for instance (that is, exhaustively describing and classifying all known examples), to be a worthwhile research project as an end in itself.

CLASSIFICATION AND TYPOLOGY

We should like to make a distinction between these two terms, and to use "classification" as a broad term referring to the general process of ordering materials or concepts by placing them in groups or classes. By "typology" we mean a much more specific process whereby empirically verifiable units—types—are derived, which are basic to future analysis.

Archeologists have always worked with types and have nearly always arrived at them implicitly or on the basis of implicit assumptions, one such fundamental assumption being that a type is a group or cluster of objects more similar to each other with respect to two or more attributes than these objects are to other groups. This typological approach to the data has not been limited to artifacts alone, but has been widely applied to many ranges of material up to and including whole cultures (for example, Willey and Phillips 1958).

At the same time there has been long-term discussion among archeologists of what constitutes a type, and what a type represents. One position is stated by Brew:

. . . 'types' are not 'found'. The student does not 'recognize' a type, he *makes* it and *puts* the object in it. Objects do not 'belong' or 'fall into' types, they are *placed* in types by the student. . . . No typological system is actually inherent in the material. . . . The classes are entities and realities only in the minds of students, they have no other existence (Brew 1946: 46).

Spaulding is opposed to this view: ". . . classification into types is a process of discovery of combinations of attributes . . . not an arbitrary procedure of the classifier" (Spaulding 1953: 305).

Our position is very similar to Spaulding's (see also Taylor 1948:142, and R. Watson N.D.) and may be summarized as follows: The particular attributes chosen to define a type may be arbitrary in the sense that they are selected from an immensely large quantity of potential attributes, but once the attributes are chosen, whether types exist or not is empirically testable. In our discussion of basic statistical procedures (pp. 140ff.), we explain how these tests are made.

This disagreement between Brew on the one hand, and Spaulding on the other, arises because Spaulding believes—as we do—that there is more in the concept of type than Brew admits. A type, to be useful, must be more than a category in a classificatory system: A type is the result of two or more attributes occurring nonrandomly with respect to one another. That is, the presence of one attribute is predictive for the presence or absence of another attribute. The concept of a type implies that there exists a relationship between two or more attributes which is *meaningful in its own right* and is more than just the common occurrence of attributes.

Spaulding disagrees with Brew because he knows that archeologists group objects with similar attributes together in ways to form types, and that, regardless of what they say ("my types are purely arbitrary"), they probably almost always produce clusters in which the attribute associations are nonrandom. The point is not that their types are incorrect, but that they have not checked to see that the attributes used to produce the types are, in fact, associated nonrandomly. Thus the real problem lies in demonstrating and making explicit the nonrandomness of the clusters. The typologist who works intuitively may be mistaken in his assessment of the attribute distributions. It may appear to him that black-on-red-painted pottery is highly associated with shell tempering, so that "Black-on-Red Shell Tempered" would seem to him to be a useful pottery type for purposes of description. But if he counts the occurrences of total black-on-red, of total shell tempering, and of black-on-red with shell temper, he might find that there is no real, statistically demonstrable relationship between them, and that therefore "Black-on-Red Shell Tempered" should not be considered a good pottery type.

In order to see clearly the relationship between attributes, one can make use of a two-by-two (or larger) table. A table of this type is made by listing the mutually exclusive attributes of the two dimensions along the sides. Each object under study can then be placed in the appropriate cell according to which attributes it possesses. Table 5-1 shows the dimension "tempering" with two mutually exclusive attributes "shell tempered" and "not shell tempered," and the dimension "pot design" with the attributes "black-on-red" and "not black-on-red." The numbers in the four cells are the numbers of pots or sherds that had each combination of attributes. The marginal totals are the total number of pots that have each attribute. In this table the marginal totals are given in percentages.

The table shows that shell temper is not more likely to occur in black-on-red pottery than in not-black-on-red pottery. In this case the pottery has been divided into four groups, but the resulting classification does not demonstrate a relationship between tem-

TABLE 5.1. DISTRIBUTION OF BLACK-ON-RED AND SHELL-TEMPERED POTTERY AT SITE 1 SHOWING RANDOM DISTRIBUTION OF THESE TWO ATTRIBUTES

	Shell tempered	Not shell tempered	%
Black-on-red	26	25	51
Not black-on-red	22	27	49
%	48	52	100

pering and design. Because there is no nonrandom association, that is, no clustering among these dimensions, we have not observed any real patterning in the data, and we have not isolated any types.

It might be asked whether the classification as it stands is not still useful in some way. It is our position that classifications of this nature will tend to obscure rather than clarify meaningful changes and relationships between attributes, and at best will not add to our understanding of the meaning of them. Further discussion of other examples will illustrate this point.

Assume the following distribution occurs at another site:

TABLE 5.2. DISTRIBUTION OF BLACK-ON-RED
AND SHELL-TEMPERED POTTERY AT SITE 2
SHOWING RANDOM DISTRIBUTION OF THESE
TWO ATTRIBUTES. NOTE THAT WHILE THE
FREQUENCIES OF THE TWO ATTRIBUTES DIFFER
FROM THOSE OF SITE 1, THERE IS NO
CHANGE IN THE NATURE OF THE RELATIONSHIP
OF THESE ATTRIBUTES

	Shell tempered	Not shell tempered	%
Black-on-red	64	16	80
Not black-on-red	16	4	20
%	80	20	100

Given the above situation, an observer might claim that Black-on-Red Shell Tempered is a useful pottery type—arbitrary or not—because the proportion of black-on-red-shell-tempered pottery changes markedly between the two sites. However, these figures do not show any statistically significant clustering of the attribute "black-on-red" with the attribute "shell tempered" (see pp. 141–42 below). There is no justification for claiming Black-on-Red Shell Tempered is a more statistically verifiable type at Site 2 than at Site 1. What has occurred is that the ratio of black-on-red pots to not-black-on-red pots has changed from 50% to 80% and at the same time shell tempered: nonshell tempered has also gone from 50% to 80%. These two independent changes have caused the change in frequency between black-on-red shell-tempered pottery at Site 1 and at Site 2.

If an archeologist had actually considered black-on-red shell tempered as a type, he would have noted that there is a difference in the pottery of the two sites, but would not have observed the real differences: (1) frequency of black-on-red pottery, and (2) frequency of use of shell temper.

To take another example, assume the following frequencies are observed at Site 3:

TABLE 5.3.   DISTRIBUTION OF BLACK-ON-RED
AND SHELL-TEMPERED POTTERY AT SITE 3
SHOWING RANDOM DISTRIBUTION OF THESE
TWO ATTRIBUTES. NOTE THAT WHILE THE
FREQUENCIES OF THE TWO ATTRIBUTES
DIFFER FROM THOSE OF SITES 1 AND 2,
THERE IS NO CHANGE IN THE NATURE OF
THE RELATIONSHIP OF THESE ATTRIBUTES

	Shell tempered	Not shell tempered	%
Black-on-red	24	6	30
Not black-on-red	56	14	70
%	80	20	100

Once more the shift in frequencies of the two attributes at the site from what they were at Sites 1 and 2 has resulted in a different frequency of the spurious pottery type "Black-on-Red Shell Tempered," but the distribution of attributes is still random.

Black-on-red shell-tempered pottery occurs in approximately the same proportions as in Site 1. On this basis, one might assume a similarity between these two sites. However, if one computes the percentage occurrence of the attributes, he can see that at Site 3 the ratio of shell tempering to nonshell tempering is 80%, and black-on-red to not-black-on-red is 20%. That is, both ratios are different from the ratios at Site 1, and by lumping the two unrelated dimensions "pot design" and "tempering" together, one may miss such important changes occurring independently within each of these dimensions.

As these examples indicate, one runs the risk of obscuring or completely missing the real relationships if, in one's analysis, he uses types that are not statistically verifiable. An analysis of the differences between black-on-red and not-black-on-red pottery at the three sites and a separate analysis of shell tempered versus nonshell tempered would reveal all the discoverable information on the changes in these attributes in a statistically verifiable manner.

The point of the discussion so far is: Given a set of attributes and a body of data to be classified, one can derive statistically verifiable, meaningful types. If no such statistically verifiable clusters exist, there is nothing to be gained by arbitrarily constructing some. The attributes one chooses to work with should reflect one's problem, whereas the types defined by those attributes should reflect the real world.

One of the most recent aspects of the debate concerning typology is the following: Given the occurrence of a statistically verified type, what does it mean? Do these verified types reflect "cultural reality?" Are they "mental templates" which existed in the minds of the makers?

The idea of the proper form of an object exists in the mind of the maker, and when this idea is expressed in tangible form in raw material, an artifact results. The idea is the mental template from which the craftsman makes the object (Deetz 1967: 45).

. . . if small size and an expanded stem are closely associated in the collection of projectile points, then our best explanation for the association is that the makers reproduced a customary pattern—that they thought of the expanding stemmed and small projectile point as a definite sort of projectile point. Further, we are permitted to suspect that the special kind of projectile had a special function or range of functions and perhaps even that the makers had a special name for the type (Spaulding 1960: 76).

Our answers to the above questions are that statistically verified types reflect patterned behavior, which may or may not correspond to mental templates. This patterned behavior can be the result of individual motor habits or other idiosyncratic behavior, or behavior defined as appropriate by the culture in question. There is no necessary correspondence between type and mental template.

The eliciting of mental templates is an interesting problem, but the concept is hard to work with for two reasons: (1) The definition of the term or concept is not widely agreed upon. For example, must culturally appropriate behavior patterns be consciously recognized by the artifact makers themselves? (2) It is difficult to test hypothetical mental templates, or to incorporate them into testable explanations.

We have stated that the attributes one uses to define types are arbitrary in the sense that, for any array of objects, there is an extremely large number of possible attributes that can be used to classify them. One's choice of attributes to use in classification is determined not by the artifacts themselves but by the purposes of the classifier. That is, such concepts as "St. Johns Polychrome" are no more or no less types than "painted bowls." However, it cannot be too strongly emphasized that it is only the selection of a few attributes from the great number possible which is, in a sense, arbitrary. Once the attributes are chosen, the types they define should be real in the sense of being statistically verifiable.

Furthermore, once the investigator has defined his problem, the attributes he chooses to work with will be anything but arbitrary. Examples follow to illustrate this point: Different problems require different intensities of typological analysis. For certain problems very gross types (that is, those based on only a few attributes) are appropriate, whereas for other problems minutely refined types (based on many attributes) may be necessary.

Hill, in testing his hypothesis concerning form and function of the rooms at Broken K Pueblo, examined the pottery from the rooms to see whether the postulated storage rooms contained more large, undecorated jars (known ethnographically as storage devices) than did the other rooms (Chapter 2: 40, 42ff.), Checking this implication necessitates only a very gross pottery typology: "large-plainware-jars" versus "not large-plainware-jars"—which can be applied with no reference to the standard southwestern pottery types present at the site (Brown Plain Corrugated, Snowflake Black-on-White, and so on).

Similarly, Deetz, in his study of Arikara ceramics, did not utilize traditional pottery types at all:

. . . only attributes here designated as stylistic were chosen. For the present study, a stylistic attribute will be defined as one which results from a choice on the part of the manufacturer from a number of possibilities, made to produce a certain effect on the finished vessel (Deetz 1965: 46).

However, he constructed a highly detailed pottery typology which —like Hill's gross pottery typology—was appropriate to his problem. He defined fifteen classes (dimensions) of attributes:

Surface Finish (plain, brushed, simple stamped, etc.)
Profile (eighteen different vessel profiles)
Shoulder-Neck Angle (angular or curved)
Lip Profile (square, pointed, braced, etc.)
Lip Decoration Technique (cord-impressed, tool-impressed, trailed, punctate, etc.)
Etc.

There are more than 150 different attributes which he applies to approximately 2500 rim sherds from his two sites. Analysis of the distributions of these attributes reveals subtle changes in the styles characteristic of the various components represented in the sherd sample. Thus, even though traditional types have been designed for this same pottery as for Hill's ceramic sample, Deetz, like Hill, found them unsuitable for his purposes and devised an entirely different kind of classification that resulted in types quite different from the traditional ones.

Another study demonstrating that different typologies are needed for different problems is Wilmsen's work with paleo-Indian-flaked stone artifacts (1968). He wished to study the functional variation and the probable uses of these artifacts. Instead of using previous typologies based on formal attributes, he defined new attributes including location of use, angle of edge, and direction of use marks. The resulting typology does not coincide with the traditional one, but by using it he was able to make important generalizations concerning the functions of these artifacts.

STATISTICAL TECHNIQUES

A scientific approach to archeological data requires the use of various statistical tecnhiques. The examples already given have demonstrated the need for these techniques at all levels of investigation, from the formulation of the research design (for instance, sampling) to artifactual analysis (for example, typology), defining relationships between artifacts (for example, factor analysis), to the testing of hypotheses about cultural process (for example, the Deetz Arikara study).

Many students of archeology are not well acquainted with all of these statistical techniques. Because the logic of the research design and of the explanations sought in some of the more recent archeological studies is intimately involved with the statistics used, it is necessary to discuss briefly some important aspects of the more common techniques. Hence, in this section we present in broad outline a selected range of these techniques. Our primary goal is to enable the reader to understand and to appraise the recent work in scientific archeology. In addition, the logic of these techniques further illustrates the logical framework of the discipline.

Statistical techniques have three general uses in archeology: First, they provide an efficient means of representation of the data; second, statistical inference is an aid to model building, that is, to formulating hypotheses or complexes of hypotheses; third, statistics can be used for testing hypotheses. However, in order to employ and understand statistical methods correctly, one must comprehend the principles of these methods and their relation to archeological data.

We consider the basic assumptions, uses, and meanings of some of the more common statistical methods rather than presenting or describing the actual computations involved. For a more thorough discussion the reader should consult such basic, general, statistical references as those of Walker and Lev (1958) and Hoel (1960, 1962). More detailed treatments can be found in Brownlee (1965) and Downie and Heath (1965), while Blalock (1960), Kolstoe (1969), and Siegel (1956) concentrate on the use of statistics in the social sciences. Daniels (1967) and Kerrich and Clarke (1967) are good examples of statistical studies by archeologists.

SCALES

Because statistical methods are related to the scales, or means of measurement, used in recording the data to be analyzed, it is necessary to examine the different scales available. There are three kinds of scales: interval, ordinal, and nominal. (Ratio scales are included with interval scales because, for our purposes, the distinction between them is not important.) Scales are discussed in Blalock (1960) and Kolstoe (1969).

The interval scale is the most familiar; it refers to any type of measurement with fixed and equal intervals between the points of the scale. Rulers, thermometers, stop watches, and so on allow measurements to be taken on interval scales. As an archeological example, assume we have three projectile points with lengths of 8 cm., 9 cm., and 10 cm. on our scale (a scale in inches would do as well). We know that the 10 cm. long point is two centimeters longer than the 8 cm. one, while the 9 cm. one is one centimeter longer. We also know that the difference between 8 cm. and 10 cm. is twice the difference between the 8 cm. and the 9 cm. An interval scale embodies the maximum amount of quantitative data about these lengths, and, in general, the most powerful statistics are those that can be used with data collected on interval scales.

The second kind of scale is the ordinal, or rank, scale. It allows one to compare items with one another, but only in a relative sense, as in Moh's Hardness Scale for minerals. Suppose we decide to rank 10 projectile points according to length and assign them numbers 1 through 10. We know that a projectile point given a value of 9 is longer than one given a value of 8, but we do not know how much longer it is. We cannot assume that there is any absolute amount of difference represented by the units of the scale. The projectile points ranked 4 and 5 could differ by 1 cm. while those ranked 9 and 10 could differ by 5 cm. It is obvious that this scale embodies less quantitative data about the projectile points than does the interval scale. Furthermore, statistical techniques that can be applied to ordinal scale data are weaker than those that can be used with interval scale data.

The third scale is the nominal scale. This scale merely places items into discrete categories without assuming anything about the differences between the categories. A nominal scale might have divisions based on shape, color, religion, or basis of descent reckoning. Any scale that measures simply the presence or absence of some attribute is a nominal scale. For example, we could divide the projectile points into two classes, "long" or "not long," by requiring any point to be at least 10 cm. to be classed "long." Such an ordering would be according to a nominal scale, and as such it conveys less quantitative data about the points than do the other two scales. Also, the statistical techniques that can be used with this kind of scale provide the least information. Table 5-4 on the following page gives a hypothetical comparison of the scales for the same imaginary ten projectile points.

In any science, the objective is to collect data in the most efficient and effective manner possible. Therefore every effort should be made to get the maximum quantity of information from the items being analyzed and, in particular, to collect the data by means of scales which convey the maximum amount of information and enable the use of the most powerful statistics. Interval scales provide the greatest quantity of statistically meaningful information, but tabulating data by use of interval scales is usually much more tedious and time-consuming than tabulation using ordinal or nominal scales. Hence, there is often a tendency to follow the path of least resistance by utilizing nominal scales. For instance, pottery lends itself easily to the use of nominal scales, and these are almost always used in pottery descriptions. However, much information is lost when one uses nominal scales, and a question arising later in the analysis that could have been answered if an interval scale had been devised and used for recording the original data might remain unanswered forever.

There is a marked uncertainty factor inherent in most archeological data (p. 112 above), quite apart from the possible randomizing effects of postaboriginal or postoccupational disturbances of many different kinds. Because of these uncertainties, the meaningful information contained in the artifacts and their distributions may be hidden or even lost. These inherent difficulties, as well as the fact that digging is destroying, make it crucial to maximize the potential of archeological data. Therefore, one should always use the most powerful scale possible in recording that data in order to recover as much as possible of the potential information.

Admittedly, for both theoretical and practical reasons, not all the data can be recorded by means of interval scales; so much ar-

TABLE 5.4.

	Interval Scale	Ordinal Scale	Nominal Scale
A	5 cm	1	short
B	5.5	2	short
C	12	8	long
D	8	5	short
E	9	6	short
F	7	4	short
G	10	7	long
H	6	3	short
I	20	10	long
J	15	9	long

cheological data will be recorded by nominal or ordinal scales. This situation means that the archeologist should be aware of existing techniques and, if possible, should develop new ones that are appropriate for these kinds of scales.

VARIABLES AND DIMENSIONS

One of the most basic questions in archeology that can be handled statistically is the relationship between two or more variables or dimensions.

The terms "dimension" and "variable" (as well as "class," "set," and "index") are often used interchangeably. A dimension is some formally defined aspect of the group of objects that is being studied. The definition must clearly specify which aspects of an object are being considered under one dimension. Every dimension is measured in terms of a scale, and the various mutually exclusive positions of the scale are attributes. "A Dimension is that aspect of a class of things or events which requires its own special measuring apparatus" (Spaulding 1960: 72).

The attributes of interval scales are defined by the establishing of the manner in which the measurement is to be made. Once this is done, the attribute is merely the value of the measurement, for example, dimension: length; attribute: 10.5 cm. For nominal and ordinal scales, mutually exclusive attributes must be defined so that the chosen aspect of any of the objects under investigation can be classified as belonging to one and only one of the attributes of the dimension. For instance, if we measured the dimension "projectile point length" and wished to have two groupings, we could define the attributes "short" and "long" as we did in the earlier example (p. 136).

One can record the attributes of a projectile point by reference to the dimensions of length, width, thickness, weight, color, number of retouch scars, and so on. On the other hand, a category such as poor or good workmanship does not describe a real or objective dimension because no one has defined what workmanship includes nor how to measure it (that is, how to decide empirically which point is "good" and which is "bad").

Dimensions may be affected by the presence or absence of other dimensions of the object. Logically speaking, this is of no particular consequence, but practically it can make interpretation of data very difficult. For example, the dimension "pottery color" could be influenced by the dimensions "firing temperature," "pot thickness," "slip thickness," "kiln form," and so on, as well as by "clay color" or "paint color." If one realizes that values in one dimension are potentially related or affected by several other dimensions, then these effects can be taken into account. If, however, one is not aware of the relations between dimensions, he may make errors in interpretation. One might classify pots from two sites as distinct pottery types in the traditional sense because of a difference in design colors, when the difference might really be only a slight change in firing temperature due to the differential availability of different fuels. That is, at both sites pots of the same type were being made, but the end products appear to be different.

As we have pointed out, for most statistical purposes, the

terms "variable" and "dimension" are equatable. However, a conceptually useful distinction can be made. Archeologists work by employing dimensions to record the characteristics of artifactual remains, but what they are really interested in is the cultural relevance of this material—that is, what it tells us about the behavior of the members of the extinct society. This behavior needs to be described in an analytic manner. In order to differentiate between culturally meaningful information on the one hand and the directly observable artifactual data from which such information is derived on the other, one can speak of *culturally meaningful variables* as contrasted with the *dimension* used to record the artifactual data. A cultural variable is logically a dimension in that it must be defined in precisely the same manner as a dimension, and a distinction between a dimension and a culturally meaningful variable can only be made at the level of interpretation, not at the mathematical level.

Some previously described studies can be used to help clarify this distinction. One could define a dimension or several dimensions concerning attributes of style, as Deetz and Longacre do. By analyzing these dimensions one could define a cultural variable, for instance, residence pattern. Similarly one can analyze many dimensions concerning tool types and define a cultural variable, agricultural autonomy, as Leone does. The study of culture process, then, would be the study of the relations between and among variables, and not the relations between and among the dimensions used to record these variables.

MEASURING RELATIONSHIPS
BETWEEN DIMENSIONS

In order to isolate the important variables in his data, the archeologist needs to know if dimensions are unrelated (independent) or related. If he decides that they are related, he needs to determine the strength and form of the relationship.

To determine whether two dimensions are independent, one can use the Chi-Squared Test.[1] This is one of the most useful statistical tools available to archeologists. The Chi-Squared Test shows the probability that the observed distribution of the data is due to chance alone. One can use the Chi-Squared Test when a set of items has been cross-classified by two different dimensions. For example, suppose for a collection of burials the sex of the individual and the pottery type found in the burial are recorded as in Table 5-5 below:

TABLE 5.5   OBSERVED FREQUENCIES

	Red Pottery	Not Red Pottery	Totals
Male	33	7	40
Female	12	8	20
Total	45	15	60

It appears that there was a tendency to bury males with red pots. One needs to know if these observed frequencies are significantly different from what might occur by chance. The Chi-Squared Test shows how much this set of frequencies differs from what would have been expected from chance association. The expected values can be determined by assuming that because $2/3$ ($40/60$) of the individuals were male and $3/4$ ($45/60$) of the pots were red, then—purely by chance—$1/2$ ($2/3 \times 3/4 = 1/2$) of all the burials should have been of males buried with red pots. Thus, of 60 burials, one would expect 30 males to be buried with red pots

[1] If the numbers are small and the table is a 2 x 2 table, the Fisher Exact Test can be used in exactly the same way as the Chi-Squared Test. All the statistics books previously referenced describe the manner in which the value of Chi-Squared is computed. See Spaulding (1953; 1960) for detailed examples of the use of Chi-Squared on archeological data.

purely by chance, that is, if there had been no tendency to bury males with red pots. The expected figures for the other squares in Table 5-6 below were found the same way.

TABLE 5.6.   EXPECTED FREQUENCIES

	Red Pots	Not Red Pots	Totals
Males	30	10	40
Females	15	5	20
Total	45	15	60

From this one can see that the observed frequencies are not far different from the expected frequencies. The value of Chi-Squared is computed and, by referring to an appropriate table, one can find that the observed distribution could have been expected to occur about one time in nine simply by chance alone, even if there were no tendency for males to be buried with red pots.

Two things must be made clear. The larger the sample, the smaller the likelihood that any deviation from the expected distribution will be due to chance alone. If 600 burials had been found in exactly the same proportions as before, the following distribution would be exhibited:

TABLE 5.7.   OBSERVED FREQUENCIES

	Red Pots	Not Red Pots	Totals
Males	330	70	400
Females	120	80	200
Total	450	150	600

This distribution would occur only one time in 1000 by chance alone.

Secondly, it should be noted that the Chi-Squared Test shows nothing about the strength of the relationship between the dimensions. If the sample size is very large, any deviation from expected values is much less likely than in a small sample. Thus, if even a small deviation occurs, the likelihood that it would be due to chance alone would be very slight. Situations can then occur where a slight deviation appears to be very significant statistically, while the actual number of cases that deviate from the expected is so small that the relationship between the two dimensions is uninteresting.

If the sample includes several thousand items, a deviation from the expected involving 30 items might be statistically significant. However, because the sample size is large, the percentage of items involved would be so small (3%) that the situation would be culturally uninteresting.

Statisticians traditionally consider a distribution significant if its chance of occurrence is less than one time in 20 (or 5% of the time). This is referred to as the ".05 level of significance." This is, of course, an arbitrary cutoff point. If hundreds of comparisons are made between large numbers of dimensions, as can now be done easily by computer, one will find that many statistical associations appear to be significant that are actually only "accidental." In theory this presents no problem because one must interpret any distribution: "No suggestion [is] made that any statistical operations [will] disclose the ultimate significance of the clusters described" (Spaulding 1954: 392). Mere statistical significance does not supply meaning no matter what the level of significance. In practice, a real problem does exist, and one must weigh the advantages between two alternate possibilities. One may miss interesting and real relationships by setting a high significance level and ignoring all distributions which do not attain it. Conversely, one may set the significance level so low he must interpret many cases that appear significant but are due only to chance.

For instance, during his study of Upper Paleolithic end scrapers, Sackett (1966) decided that the traditional .05 level would probably eliminate too many real relationships because of the nature of the sample, so he chose a .10 level. Although he risked including some spurious relationships in his results, the gains are worth the possible additional analytical effort. This is an important point, because of the difficulties inherent in archeological data (pp. 112 and 137 above). There are many gaps between the behavior of the people who once occupied a site and our description and interpretation based on the altered and selected debris that resulted and remains in the archeological record from that behavior. Flint can break where it was not intended to and spatial distributions of artifacts can be modified by noncultural factors. This does not mean the data are unusable but it does mean that statistical procedures must be modified accordingly, as Sackett has done.

The Chi-Squared Test can be used with any scale, although other, more powerful methods exist for making this kind of test with ordinal or interval scales.

Once one decides that a relationship between two or more dimensions is not due to chance, he will probably want to learn something about the nature of the relationship. Analyses of this kind made on two dimensions are called "correlation analyses" and "regression analyses." If there are more than two dimensions to be considered, the techniques are generally called "multivariate analyses." Some of the techniques of multivariate analysis are multiple correlation analysis, multiple regression analysis, and factor analysis.

Let us first consider the two-dimension case. Correlation analysis can be done with interval, ordinal, and nominal scales, but different statistics must be used for each scale. Regression analysis can be done with interval scales, but there are no comparable techniques for ordinal or nominal scales.

Regression analysis shows the form taken by a relationship between two dimensions and enables one to derive an equation of this relationship. In this sense it is a predictive statement because, given a value of one dimension, one is able to predict (within a certain margin of error) the value of the other dimension. Regression analysis can be demonstrated by first plotting all the values of the two dimensions on a graph, then finding a line that minimizes the square of the distance of each point from the line. A straight line is usually found, so this technique is called linear regression analysis. It is possible, however, to seek more complex lines.

An example of linear regression (after Spaulding 1960) is measuring the lengths and widths of our same projectile points on an interval scale and plotting the results. (Fig. V-3) One can determine the regression and plot it, all on the same graph. This particular regression equation, width $= .6 \times$ length, shows that for every centimeter that length increases, there is .6 cm. of increased width. For any length one can predict what width should be found. It is possible to draw some sort of line through the points on the diagram even if they are randomly scattered over the graph, so one needs to know how closely these points fit the line. This is really asking whether the dimensions are related or independent.

To answer this question one uses a measure of correlation. If

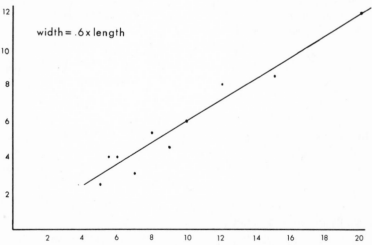

Figure V-3: Regression Graph of 10 Projectile Points

interval scales are used as above, a statistic invented by Pearson and called "r" can be used. In essence, r tells us how close the points of the graph are to occurring in a straight line. Thus one could have two different sets of data with different regression lines but the same value of r.

Most measures of correlation (including Pearson's r) range in value from -1 to $+1$. If r has a value of less than 0.5, most statisticians feel that too few of the points are close to the regression line and thus that the line is not a very good indication of the relationship between the dimensions. This is a completely arbitrary cutoff point, but it has become a rule of thumb in the social sciences. It is certainly possible that in some cases an r of less than 0.5 would be meaningful and would contribute to the understanding of a particular relationship. Note, however, that this is only for r; measures of correlation in general are not comparable, and it is wrong to require that all measures of correlation have a fixed cutoff point. The 0.5 rule of thumb is not usable for any other measure. For interval scales the regression line gives the equation expressing the form of the relationship between two dimensions, while the r coefficient shows how closely the data conform to this equation.

The assumptions behind the statistics based on interval scales require the sample data to follow certain known distributions (for example, normal distributions) and also require one to be able to estimate certain parameters (for example, mean and standard deviation) of the original universe that was sampled. Data measured by means of ordinal and nominal scales do not allow one to assume the distributions or the parameters required of many statistics used on interval scale data; the latter are usually referred to as parametric statistics. Statistics applied to data measured by ordinal and nominal scales must be of different kinds and these are usually referred to as nonparametric statistics.

Two nonparametric measures of association that can be used with ordinal scales are Spearman's Rho and Kendall's Tau. One uses them to measure how closely the ranking by one dimension compares with the ranking by another. Different methods are employed to do this, and the value of the Rho coefficient is usually not the same as the Tau coefficient for the same set of data. More importantly, there is no way to determine the precise meaning of a given value of these measures. In particular, one cannot assume that by going from a value of .3 to a value of .6 there is twice the correlation.

For nominal scales other correlation measures exist (see Siegel 1956 for statistical techniques based on nominal and ordinal data). Some of these are the Contingency Coefficient, Cramer's V, and Goodman and Krushnal's Tau, all of which range from 0 to 1. The first two start with the values of the Chi-Squared that have been determined for the data and take into account the effect of sample size. However, the values of the coefficients reflect only the amount of deviation from the expected values and not the effects of sample size. The Goodman and Krushnal Tau is based on a probability model and is, theoretically at least, more easily interpretable. These correlation measures, like those for ordinal and interval scales, show the strength of a relationship and not its form. In general one cannot use a measure of correlation to describe the form of a relationship between two dimensions. It might also be noted here that a strong degree of association does not demonstrate a causal relationship between dimensions.

MULTIVARIATE ANALYSIS

In the case where there are more than two dimensions, methods similar to those just discussed can be employed. For interval scales multiple regression analysis, especially multiple linear regression and multiple correlation analysis, are logical continuations of the two-dimension cases. When ordinal scales are used, some multiple correlation can be done. There exist for interval scales, however, the additional techniques of factor analysis and proximity analysis (L. Binford and S. Binford 1966; Cowgill 1968). Although factor analysis is being more widely used, it is not well understood and hence merits some discussion.

Multiple factor analysis, or simply factor analysis, is a technique which begins with a large number of measures and reduces them to a few hypothetical basic variables. First, data are recorded by means of a series of dimensions, then the values of each dimension are correlated with those of every other dimension. It is then assumed that there is really a smaller set of variables that can explain the correlations observed, because the original dimensions are probably each measures of several different variables at the same time. By finding these new variables, which are labeled factors, one simplifies the empirical situation. These factors can produce a difference in representations that is easier to comprehend, and it is in the hope of this result that the archeologist uses them.

Fewer factors than the original number of dimensions (ideally, half as many) can usually account for most of the original correlations, but not for all of them. The portions of the correlations unaccounted for are labeled "residuals."

It is next necessary to interpret these factors. The original factors are not unique, but are dependent on the order in which the data were analyzed; a process called "rotation" is employed to modify the solution. Rotations transform the factors until they correlate with the original dimensions in a way that will allow us to understand what the factors represent. Usually a rotation is performed so that one factor becomes very highly correlated with one of the original measures. One can assume that the original measure and the factor account for the same effect, thus one can interpret the factor as being essentially the same as the measure with which it is highly associated. Other factors will be changed by this initial rotation and might still be difficult to interpret. Holding the first factor in place, one rotates the other factors so that the second factor will coincide closely with some other original measure and can be interpreted in the same manner as the first. This process is repeated with the remaining factors.

Various assumptions can be made in performing the rotations. One can assume that the underlying factors that really account for the observed correlations in the original data are independent of one another. In graphical terms, this means that the factors would be graphed at right angles to one another, and hence they are labeled orthogonal. This kind of rotation is then an orthogonal rotation. The factors produced by an orthogonal rotation are usually quite different from those produced by other kinds of rotations. There is a tendency in many of the social sciences to use only orthogonal rotations. However, anthropological research designs do not necessarily require one to assume independent factors, and thus to use orthogonal rotations exclusively. Research designs including possibly related factors are also feasible, and nonorthogonal rotations would be required in these cases. Because computer programs exist that allow either type of rotation to be performed (as well as variations that will not be considered here), there is no a priori need to prefer one type of rotation over another.

Whatever rotation is used should be justified on the basis of the data being analyzed and the question being asked. Even after rotation, one must still interpret the factors and decide just what effects or causes they represent. In general, deciding what factors really measure is logically on the level of hypothesis formulation, and the explanation of the factors cannot be based solely on the factor analysis. Instead, these, like other hypotheses, should be tested by independent means. It is equally possible that, having already formulated a hypothesis, one could employ factor analysis as one of the means of testing this hypothesis.

In this section we have stressed the various scales of measurement and the analyses of relationships between different dimensions or measurements on these scales. This is, of course, only a small part of the potential statistical analysis which can and should be performed on archeological data. These topics are discussed here because they arise frequently, yet are generally less well understood than those such as means, standard deviations, normal curves, and so on. The distinction made between different scales is important because a great deal of archeological data is represented with these scales. It should be stressed once more that the most powerful scale, the interval scale, should be used whenever possible.

THE CONCEPTUAL FRAMEWORK
FOR AN EXPLICITLY SCIENTIFIC ARCHEOLOGY

In closing this chapter on selected aspects of archeological method, we wish to consider the present lack of consensus within the field concerning a number of basic methodological and epistemological issues. These issues must be discussed and some decisions reached if prehistoric archeology is to be placed upon a sound scientific footing. The most basic problem is the epistemological one: How does one attain knowledge of the past; and what is the justification for wanting to do so? In Chapters 3, 4, and 5, however, we have assumed consensus on that issue in favor of explicitly scientific archeology (possible justifications for this approach are further discussed in Chapter 6), and have been concerned with some aspects of archeological method: How does one proceed validly and efficiently toward the objectives of explicitly scientific archeology?

One of the most pressing problems here is that of commonly agreed upon basic assumptions: What lawlike generalizations drawn from the social sciences can be taken as givens (for example, can we all agree that in a matrilocal society women learn to decorate pots from their mothers and grandmothers and undertake very little innovating or copying outside this context?), and what ones need to be tested and confirmed before we as archeologists use them? There should be open discussion of the status of these generalizations and active testing of them.

Further, there is the question of adequate confirmation of such generalizations and of other hypotheses. What quality and quantity of results should be generally accepted as adequate confirmation (see pp. 46–49 above)? Again, these questions can be resolved only by discussion and debate among concerned archeologists.

There has never been a very thorough consensus among field archeologists—especially those working in the Old World—on all major, practical aspects of excavation technique, and there has been and is considerable difference of opinion regarding the appropriateness of various digging and recording techniques in given situations. There are some common understandings in these matters, however, and the disagreements do not seem especially significant when compared to those potentially inherent in an even greater problem of standardization now arising which pertains to analytic procedures. More and more attention is being given to computer-aided statistical analyses; there is strong pressure on archeologists to employ these techniques in which very few of them at the present time have received any formal training. For example, there is increasing use of factor analysis, but one cannot assume that all professional archeologists know when and how to apply this technique to their data in the way one can assume a professional archeologist knows how and when to apply the techniques of flotation or fine-screening to his site.

The significance and logic of many analytical procedures is coming into question, such as, for example, the nature and use of typologies. There has traditionally been much concern with archeological (and ethnographic) typology, but marked progress has not been made. If, however, we adopt an explicitly scientific framework as in pp. 126–34 above, much of the confusion and difficulty should disappear.

In spite of these current uncertainties, we believe an operational consensus will emerge if archeologists deliberately set themselves to the task of establishing and maintaining discussion and ◦xchange of opinions concerning the various problems. Once archeologists accept the basic scientific assumption that the most adequately confirmed current hypothesis is simply the best approximation to truth, they are freed from deep personal commitment to entrenched theoretical positions. Then opinions and hypothetical formulations need not be evaluated primarily on the basis of the personal abilities of the person presenting them, but rather on the nature of the data themselves. Final assessment of these recent developments in archeology will be based on the degree of success we have in attaining agreement on objectives and methods, and in utilizing those methods to produce substantive and valuable published results.

CHAPTER SIX

𐰭𐰭𐰭𐰭𐰭𐰭𐰭𐰭𐰭𐰭𐰭𐰭𐰭𐰭𐰭𐰭𐰭𐰭𐰭𐰭𐰭𐰭𐰭𐰭𐰭𐰭𐰭𐰭𐰭𐰭𐰭𐰭𐰭𐰭

ARCHEOLOGY AS SOCIAL SCIENCE: PROBLEMS AND PROSPECTS

WE HAVE EXAMINED the logical structure of a scientific archeology and the general methods of excavation, analysis, and interpretation appropriate to such a discipline. In this concluding chapter we will touch upon some particularly pressing problems which must be solved by the practitioners of scientific archeology, and we will then consider some of the general aspects of archeology explicitly conceived as a social science.

THE ORGANIZATION
OF ARCHEOLOGICAL FIELD WORK

Probably the single most obvious trend in contemporary archeology is toward long-term, thoroughly interdisciplinary studies of whole regions. In the past it was usual for a single archeologist to mastermind all planning and operations at his site. Excavation and analysis were essentially a one-man show, and every archeologist was expected to be very much a jack-of-all-trades. He took charge of mapping the site, recording the excavations (including photography), analyzing the results, and organizing the publication. The one-man show era is now past. Braidwood pioneered the modern, cooperative, interdisciplinary field program in his 1954–1955 Iraq-Jarmo Project (Braidwood and Howe 1960) in which the full-time staff included a geologist, a zoologist, and a paleoethno-botanist, in addition to two archeologists, two archeological field assistants, and a ceramicist. Interdisciplinary efforts focusing on whole regions rather than single sites have now become more common (MacNeish 1967; Hole, Flannery, and Neely 1969), but as archeologists become interested in more subtle and complex problems, the difficulties of organizing large-scale, intensive, long-term, interdisciplinary field programs becomes immense. Struever has argued compellingly for a radical alteration in the institutional structure within which archeology operates. He says that marked change has occurred in archeological theory over the past twenty years without corresponding changes in the scope and complexity of actual field operations.

Manpower, equipment, specialists and other elements that must be combined in the successful execution of archeological research are today organized for the most part on a level no higher than they were in the 1930s. The occasional, large-scale collaborative projects are notable exceptions. Until the intellectual advances of these past few years are matched by advances in actual research performance—in part through changes in the institutional structure within which archeology operates—much of the potential contribution of the new concepts and methods for dealing with specific problems like the description of subsistence-settlement systems, assessing prehistoric population densities, and analyzing the structure of interaction spheres, cannot be realized (Struever 1971:18).

The leadership of the project would be in the hands of several archeologists and at least a few collaborating specialists who are as interested and involved in the major problem being investigated as are the archeologists. Although we think it is important for archeologists and collaborators with different interests and abilities to work together, it is essential that the entire effort not be completely compartmentalized and broken down into an assembly line form of production. There must be a few people (archeologists and full-time collaborating specialists) who view the project in its entirety and are able to evaluate and plan research involving data from several different fields. That is, we believe that every stage of the research—from formulation of the problem, of the hypotheses derived from it, of the test implications to be checked, and of the succeeding field work and analyses—should be conceived and handled as a completely cooperative affair among the full-time collaborators (archeologists working with botanists, ethnologists, zoologists, geologists, physical anthropologists, and so on). The ideal archeological project of the future should also have ready access to the services of a variety of technicians who might be consulted about plant and animal remains, the identification of raw materials used to manufacture artifacts, details of the history or ethnohistory of the region, the source areas of imported items, the nature of the prehistoric climate and land forms, or certain aspects of the social and political organization of contemporary local communities.

There should also be excavation technicians who might be called in to exercise their special skills as bulldozer operators, flotation experts, burial experts, and so on.

Finally, it is important for the members of the project to integrate their activities into the local region as much as possible. It is unnecessary and unfair for an archeological project to move into a region, carry out the research, and depart without ever establishing meaningful contact with the local inhabitants. If the work is being done in a foreign country, cooperative arrangements should be made with professors and students at local universities or other research institutions. Whether at home or abroad, attention should be given to relationships with the local population, and care should be taken to communicate important research to the interested public. The prehistory of a region is as much a part of its heritage as its flora and fauna, and the archeological record of past lifeways should be carefully protected.

PUBLICATION OF ARCHEOLOGICAL REPORTS

A number of points should be made concerning publication of archeological investigations. The first has been made many times before: A report should be published as soon as possible after the excavation is completed.

Participants in the ideal archeological project referred to in the previous section will be in an excellent position to get their results out quickly because much of the basic analysis has been completed in the field, and because the collaborators are working closely together, continuously exchanging data and ideas. Another result of this close collaboration is that the written contributions of these various experts are integral to the entire report, and they are not included as detachable appendices bearing no direct relationship to the main body of the publication.

A more general and much more pressing problem than either time lag or specialists' reports, however, is that of the basic nature of the report itself. Should one strive to publish large quantities of detailed description or primary data, or should he emphasize interpretation of this data? The former is now customary: Emphasis is on description, increasing detail, and more measurements, with only a small percentage of the report given to interpretation of the material described.

The goal of archeologists utilizing this procedure is to publish all the necessary data to vindicate the conclusions reached by the investigator. However, as archeologists undertake more intensive and long-term projects involving more and more interdisciplinary work, and as publishing and labor costs rise, this form of publication will become increasingly unwieldy and finally impossible to pursue.

At present, then, there are three possibilities:

1. Total publication: Publish all the data recovered together with the conclusions and interpretations based on them.

2. Summary interpretation: Publish the conclusions only—a reconstruction of prehistoric lifeways at the site excavated —and little or no data per se.

3. Problem-oriented publication: Publish a discussion of the problem upon which the excavation focused, and present its solution, or new insights gained into it, with only enough data from the site excavated to support the argument.

As noted, total publication is the more or less accepted standard of publication now, but we predict that this procedure will very soon become so costly in time, effort, and money that it will be impossible to follow.

The difficulties resulting from choice of one of the other methods of publication are well illustrated by P. E. L. Smith's recent review of an important archeological report: *Prehistory and Human Ecology of the Deh Luran Plain* by Frank Hole, Kent Flannery, and James Neely (1969). Smith voices the dilemma as follows:

This book calls for a split-level review: as the exposition of an archeological approach with its subsequent hypotheses, and as a descriptive excavation report. It is a pity that in the process of illustrating how productive and stimulating an ecological approach can be in archeology the authors have written a rather less than satisfactory excavation report. Indeed, the defects shown here raise some important questions concerning archeological technique, theory, and strategy. The real trouble is that the report fails to present all the information one expects to find in a modern and final description of several important sites. Researchers who wish to consult it for certain kinds of information, or from viewpoints somewhat different from those the authors have considered important, will find the work unnecessarily difficult or even impossible (Smith 1970: 708).

Smith approves of the theoretical orientation of the Hole, Flannery, and Neely report, but, from his own point of view, finds definite shortcomings in it:

Since archeologists must rely on very detailed descriptions and presentations of all the data observed which enter into the investigator's interpretations, it is necessary for final reports to be as exhaustive as is humanly possible.

A colleague who has read this book argues that its defects are inherent in research which is oriented to a single approach. I don't agree with him. Much in this book is good, and the weaknesses were avoidable (Smith 1970: 708, 709).

In Smith's opinion, Hole, Flannery, and Neely have produced a report which is too problem-oriented. Although we do not think the report so far from the total publication standard as Smith apparently does, we can use this example to make the following point: From Smith's viewpoint, the Hole, Flannery, and Neely position fits that described earlier (Chapter 5, pp. 114ff.) in our discussion of relevant data, but—as Smith indicates—is not entirely satisfactory to archeologists with differing interests who make different demands of the archeological record. On the other hand, a report full of detail describing artifactual categories of significance for comparative purposes is not entirely satisfactory to the problem-oriented archeologists, who may require information not even recognized as data by the excavator, and hence not recorded and published.

Some of these difficulties—as discussed elsewhere (pp. *viii–xii* and end of Chapter 6)—stem from the differences in basic orientation among archeologists, but much of this conflict of interest could be ameliorated if each site or region were published in several ways. This could be done if archeologists would establish a microcard or microfilm file, into which they could put their basic data so that it is available in its entirety to all other researchers. Such a microcard file was established in 1960 by the Society for American Archeology. It is called the Archives of Archeology and is now published jointly by the Society and the University of Wisconsin. To date, twenty-eight titles have been published and the cost is low (less than one cent per page, seventy to eighty pages per card), but the program should be expanded and pressure brought to bear on excavators to ensure their cooperation. Given the existence of such a data file, the archeologist need not choose between publishing one monolithic volume which attempts to include all the data, as well as an interpretation of it, *or* producing one definitive journal article which is a closely reasoned theoretical formulation based on the results of excavation and analyses but which contains very little data. He could choose not to publish the bulk of the data at all, but could produce a problem-oriented report, or a summary interpretation, or both. This could result in the publication of a site report, as well as a series of theoretically oriented journal articles, but the bulk of the data would remain in the microcard or microfilm file.

ARCHEOLOGY AS A SOCIAL SCIENCE

The purpose of this book is to provide a synthesis, or coherent summary, of what scientific procedure in archeology means. Accordingly, we have described and discussed in Chapters 2, 3, and 4 what is logically entailed if archeologists explicitly adopt the scientific method with the goal of formulating and testing hypothetical laws and explanations which will enable them to understand past events and processes, and to use this information in formulating and testing hypothetical laws and explanations about present human behavior and cultural processes.

We do not regard the recent emphasis on scientific method and explanation in archeology to be a fad. We see it rather as the culmination of a long development within the field, some of the earlier phases of which are shown in the writings of Steward and Setzler (1938), John W. Bennett (1943), Walter W. Taylor (1948), and Albert C. Spaulding (1953). However, this is not to say that we think now all archeologists should and must be scientists. There is no more reason for all archeologists to be scientists than for all historians to be sociologists, psychologists, or anthropologists. But archeology as a social science *is* distinct from archeology as art history, for instance, and the practitioners of the former will have different goals and problems from those of the latter. Our purpose in writing this book is to present what we take to be the most important characteristics of a model of archeology as a social science, and we will now consider some of the general aspects of this topic.

Social science is logically no different from any other kind of science. Anything that is empirically observable or sensible can be treated scientifically. Present human behavior is empirically observable, and past human behavior may also be empirically observed wherever the results of that behavior—cultural debris and its spatial distribution—are preserved. The hallmark of the physical sciences is the employment of controlled experiments. The subject matter of the social sciences—human behavior, past and present—is not amenable to that method of study, but can be made the subject of an equally effective method utilizing controlled observations. This method has enabled astronomy to become a mature, predictive science without the aid of actual experiments.

Thus, though social science is not logically different from other sciences, it is practically more difficult than the physical and many of the biological sciences. In the first place, as just noted, it is difficult and often impossible to experiment with the subject matter (people). Hence, controlled investigations of various kinds and diverse observations in many times and places are necessary to provide sources of independent data for testing hypothetical laws and explanations.

In the second place, there is a great deal of variation in human behavior, probably more than in the behavior of any other animal. That is, an individual's behavior must be very highly deviant before negative selective pressures affect it. This means the behavioral norms and their ranges of variation are more difficult to delimit for human beings than is the behavioral norm of a bee dance, for instance, because the range of individual variation in human behavior can be and is so much greater. This is partly because human beings, like mammals in general, are the result of a long period of positive selection for behavioral adaptability rather than for behavioral specialization. A highly significant aspect of this adaptability is the buffering or cushioning effect of culture, which is a form of learned behavior developed to a much greater degree in humans than in any other animal, and which acts as a highly efficient adaptive mechanism.

Anthropology as a social science may be defined as that discipline whose practitioners are interested in formulating and testing hypothetical laws enabling explanations and prediction of human cultural behavior. Anthropologically oriented archeologists may then be viewed as anthropologists who have developed techniques and skills focused on the explanation of past human behavior as it is preserved in the archeological record.[1] Archeologists operating as anthropologists and social scientists want to explain the archeological record, and also to use archeological data and the archeological record to test hypothetical laws of cultural process. For instance, Longacre is interested in the interrelationship of social organization and economy over time, and especially during a period of environmental stress (drought) (Longacre 1968: 89). To test his hypotheses concerning this interrelationship, he must be able to recognize in the archeological record the social organization before, during, and after stress. As a first step in comprehending the social organization, he devised the design-element distribution study discussed in Chapter 2 (p. 36). The results indicated, as one major conclusion, that the social organization at the time of occupation included postmarital residence of couples with or near the wife's female relatives. This conclusion not only helps explain some of the particulars of the archeological record

---

[1] This is true, but it should be pointed out that nonanthropologically oriented archeologists may use many of the same basic excavation procedures and techniques for different ends (art history, for instance).

at the Carter Ranch site but it also advances Longacre's study of culture process in the region.

In some cases, the archeological record may not be the best place to test laws or explanations, even if the methods of observation have been worked out. Some problems may be more efficiently handled by the use of ethnographic, sociological, or historical data. For other problems, however, the archeological record may be extremely helpful or may furnish information available nowhere else. If the problem has to do with hunting-gathering groups, for example, use of archeological data on extinct hunters and gatherers in various parts of the world will greatly increase the sample size over that available among living peoples.

Finally, there is one area which is uniquely exploitable by archeologists: Only archeological data can be used to test laws about various aspects of prehistoric cultural evolution because only archeology has access to the long time-spans necessary for the formulating and testing of hypothetical laws concerning the development of technology, social and political organization, art forms, and so on in nonliterate societies. Historians, like ethnographers, have access to a limited number of societies only, and within those societies can work only in those realms where records were made and preserved. This situation has been recognized by archeologists:

Given the enormous time depth with which only archaeology is prepared to deal, what can we learn of the changing relation between man, society and culture on the one hand and environment on the other; what of the generalized cultural processes . . . which, because of the bearing of this time factor . . . can be examined in no other way . . . (Braidwood 1967: 226).
(See also Spaulding 1968: 38, quoted on p. 31 here.)

The uniqueness of archeology's contribution to the study of evolutionary phenomena is discussed in some detail in a recent paper by R. Watson:

From the viewpoint of the philosophy of science, is there anything special about archeology as a science? This raises the question of whether there are any lawlike generalizations that can be specifically or uniquely originated, tested, and confirmed in archeology. The answer is that, generally, archeology is parasitic on other sciences, but that its data are the only data that can be used to test and to confirm generalizations about evolutionary change in human societies, and hence that the uniqueness of archeology as a science is that it considers evolutionary phenomena. So if archeology is anything, it is *evolutionary* anthropology (Watson N.D.: 1).

The above discussion raises some questions about the nature of archeological theory.

ARCHEOLOGICAL THEORY

A scientific theory, formally speaking, is a body of related laws. Theories are usually constructed when there are many confirmed laws in a science, but they may also be hypothetical and open to test as an entirety. The laws of a theory can be axiomatized, so that lawlike theorems can be deduced from them, although it is not necessary to a theory that the laws that make it up be organized in axiomatic form. When they are, however, it is to be emphasized that before the theorems deduced from an axiomatized theory can themselves be accepted as laws, they must be empirically confirmed. Testing the empirical truth of theorems deduced from an axiomatized theory is, in fact, the primary way of testing the truth of the theory.

The question arises as to whether there is a large enough body of confirmed laws about the subject matter of archeology to merit their grouping as an independent body of archeological theory.

The answer is a qualified no. Most of the laws now used in archeological explanations are from other social sciences such as anthropology, sociology, and psychology. Many of these laws have been or can be tested (checked under diverse sets of conditions) by archeological data, but they are not usually "archeological" themselves; that is, they were initially derived and tested as psychological, sociological, or anthropological laws. For example, the Longacre and Hill studies are based on laws like the following: People continue to make artifacts the way they were taught, whether they live their lives in one community—as women do in a matrilocal society—or whether after maturity they move to another community—as men do in a matrilocal society. If such laws were to be explicitly formulated in archeological terms, they would often parallel those existing in other, nonhistorical social sciences, or could be as well or better tested in existing communities than by appeal to the archeological record. Therefore, it is probably best to rely overtly on the established laws and theories of the other social sciences when these are available and appropriate.

To one area of interest, however, archeology can make a unique contribution. The laws and details of prehistoric human and cultural evolution can be derived from and tested only by reference to the archeological (and paleontological) record. Archeologists can formulate and test hypothetical laws about prehistoric cultural evolution, for example, that are necessarily independent of those in other sciences that derive from different subject matter. These "archeological" laws about the processes of human and cultural evolution can be used to explain details of human history. Perhaps enough such laws have now been confirmed to build such a theory (but probably not to axiomatize it). Such a theory would be relatively independent of those of the other social sciences, even though pertaining to the same type of material: people and culture. And it would be directly subordinate to a comprehensive theory of evolution that comprises all evolutionary processes.

Thus there is in a sense an "archeological theory," although it might be better characterized as evolutionary anthropology (see R. Watson N.D.). Its subject matter is unique enough, and human and cultural evolution is of such scientific and intrinsic interest that there is certainly an essential nomothetic role to be played by archeologists (see the discussion of Trigger below).

Finally, some people take archeological theory to refer to the methods and techniques of excavation and analysis. There is such a body of rules and procedures, but they are probably not independent of the methods of paleontology, geology, and engineering. They vary from commonsense procedures in dirt archeology to sophisticated statistical techniques as described above. Although it is not logically objectionable to group all these general rules together into a body to be called "archeological theory," this theory obviously does not have a content of the sort discussed in the preceding paragraphs, and so it surely would best be referred to simply as the set of methods or procedures used in archeology.

Will there ever be enough purely archeological laws to justify the organization of an independent archeological theory? Obviously not to the extent that the totality of archeology is eclectic, necessarily utilizing laws of all other sciences in its explanations of human and cultural history and prehistory. But just as obviously, we are already on our way to the development of an independent and scientifically respectable theory of evolutionary anthropology.

THE AIMS OF PREHISTORY

The discussion on pp. 159–65 above sketches an idealized situation and represents only one position within nonhumanistically oriented archeology. What should be the objectives of archeological research?

Archeologists have often viewed an interest in formulating and testing hypothetical laws as conflicting with and antithetical to an interest in collecting and describing data. Thus the field is sometimes simplistically described as consisting of old or traditional or historical (collecting data) versus new or progressive or scientific (testing laws) archeology. As Trigger (1970) notes in a recent article on the goals of prehistoric archeology, a number of self-professed new archeologists have made strong statements to the effect that archeology should be or must be an objective comparative science, or social science, devoted to nomothetic, that is, generalizing, goals. Trigger also finds in these statements "varying degrees of hostility" toward the traditional approach to prehistory.

There certainly are differences among the interests and emphases at stake, but each is a legitimate interest or emphasis if the researchers are clear as to what they are doing, which tack they are taking, and why. Moreover, the two procedures are necessarily complementary. These new archeologists have every right to criticize those who claim to be doing processual or scientific archeology but are not, and the particularists have every right to criticize processualists who insist that all archeology must be pursued according to their definition.

It is extremely important to see these issues as clearly as possible, and—though we disagree with some of the things he says—we welcome Trigger's article as a contribution to the dialogue essential for the forging of the consensus on goals and methods referred to elsewhere (Chapters 1, 2, 4, and pp. 171–72 below). Some of the main points he makes deserve discussion here. (1) We note first that Trigger—just as we do—regards the recent emphasis on scientific method in archeology as a natural and healthy development:

Archaeologists are now faced with the demands of an articulate minority that they should use their findings, alongside ethnological data, as building blocks in a single generalizing science of culture. I see this not as an erratic demand, but rather as the logical culmination of one line of thought, that has long been implicit in American archaeology. Unfortunately, the objections that have been raised against this point of view have not succeeded so far in coming to grips with the main issues. Instead, they have revealed that a great lack of clear thinking about major theoretical issues lies behind the facade of much traditional archaeology (Trigger 1970: 28).

(2) The second point concerns the differences between history and science and between ideographic and nomothetic objectives. We

agree with Trigger's assertion that history is not now and probably never was devoted to pure description of facts, and that the aims of history are to employ general rules (that is, general laws) to gain an understanding of individual situations, and "to explain individual situations in all their complexity" (Trigger 1970: 30). In his discussion of science and particularly of social science, however, he seems to be saying that though historians can and do pursue both particularizing and generalizing objectives, social scientists are devoted solely to extracting recurrent variables and to stating general relationships without ever using these general rules to explain concrete situations. He expresses this opinion by saying that history is ideographic and the social sciences nomothetic, and by defining these terms to mean that historians are primarily interested in explaining individual situations by use of general laws, whereas social scientists are concerned only with formulating general laws about human behavior and culture processes but do not use the confirmed laws to explain the phenomena of their subject.

(3) From this position he goes on to characterize archeology as an ideographic discipline and, though he probably does not believe it, he often seems to be saying that because of the nature of its data prehistoric archeology cannot or should not be included among the (nomothetic) social sciences.

We comment with respect to (2) that without reference to generalizations about human behavior no narrative or history about humans could be told; hence, no historian can explain the past without persistent appeal to such generalizations. Trigger clearly implies this himself. In order to explain particulars one must have general laws under which to subsume them. And, conversely, the main practical justification for attempting to derive such general laws is so that they can be used to explain (and to predict) human behavior and the dynamics of cultural process. The acquiring of knowledge about anything means continuous feedback between generalizing (nomothetic) and particularizing (ideographic) processes (see Steward 1949: 1–3). The scientifi-

cally oriented archeologists to whom Trigger refers as being somewhat hostile to traditionalists are combatting the prevailing but
often implicit emphasis on particularizing which has resulted in
fuzzy thinking or no thinking at all about nomothetic objectives,
with consequent lack of progress toward understanding [2] of the
subject matter.

Although there are, within any science, individual researchers more interested in formulating general laws than in applying
them (and vice-versa), the goal of any science is to use general
laws and theories (the latter being complexes of related general
laws) to explain and predict the behavior of its subject matter. Explanation cannot be achieved in the absence of confirmed general
laws. Therefore both history and social science inevitably utilize
both approaches, and the point Trigger must intend is the debatable one that the primary emphasis of most social scientists is
usually nomothetic rather than ideographic. That is, he thinks they
are more concerned with the use of particulars to derive general
laws than with the details of or the explanation of the particulars
per se. Trigger adds that in history the emphases are reversed:
Primary concern is with describing and explaining the particulars.
Trigger agrees these particulars cannot be explained without reference to general laws of human behavior and cultural process of
which—we would add—there are as yet very few that are confirmed, though there is a large body of implicit and untested commonsense generalizations. Historians can explain the past only by
persistent appeal to such implicit, untested laws and commonsense
explanations. Hence, historians—like all social scientists—must
be at least in part consciously concerned with the confirmation and
confirmability of the generalizations they appeal to in giving explanations in history.

Trigger's main point ([3] above) is that prehistoric archeology should be predominantly historical or ideographic, not nom-

---

[2] By which we always mean the attaining of a body of general laws enabling explanation and prediction of the phenomena being studied.

othetic. Logically, there is no reason why this should be true. Any given series of empirically observable phenomena can be studied to obtain either nomothetic or ideographic results. But practically speaking there may be reasons why certain data are more amenable to an ideographic approach than to a nomothetic one, and this is apparently the argument Trigger wishes to make about prehistoric archeology. He says:

> The desire to make nomothetic objectives the primary goal of archeology is rather like a biologist attempting to use the fossilized remains of *Merychippus* to study the circulation of the blood, or the skulls of juvenile and adult australopithecines to work out general principles of bone development. Both of these problems are clearly best studied on living animals in the laboratory . . . (Trigger 1970: 35).

The latter part of his statement is true: It would certainly be better to study blood circulation or bone development in living experimental animals than in fossil specimens (although fossils are essential if one is interested in the evolution of either), but his 1:1 analogical equation of this specific example to the whole question of nomothetic and ideographic objectives in archeology (and in biology, for that matter) is misleading. In effect he is saying that one cannot study the general aspects of circulation of the blood in fossil remains of *Merychippus,* and that by analogy archeological data are irrelevant to the nomothetic study of culture process and must be utilized only ideographically. In reply, we stress that—as discussed above—archeological data provide the *only* means for investigating culture process over long time periods, and hence are certainly not irrelevant to the nomothetic aspects of such an investigation. Furthermore, as noted above (p. 162), use of the archeological record as a source of independent data for testing general laws from the other social sciences is potentially of great nomothetic importance.

The question of which (if either) emphasis should dominate prehistoric archeology—nomothetic or ideographic—is certainly debatable and cannot be resolved without thorough discussion.

Advocates of the nomothetic emphasis have only begun full-scale research, and observers are justified in reserving judgment temporarily. However, there is no question but that the data of prehistory provide the only information available on which to base generalizations about culture process and human behavior over very long prehistoric time periods, and that they are a potential source of independent evidence for the testing of a multitude of hypothetical laws.

Finally, it is possible that some part of the dispute does not really concern the relations of nomothetic to ideographic goals, but reflects what various archeologists have been trained to do, are good at doing, and like to do. Trigger clearly prefers the ideographic aspects of archeology; the self-professed new archeologists prefer the nomothetic. Trigger appears to be alarmed and disturbed at the threat by highly vocal champions of a nomothetic emphasis (who sometimes overstate their position in an attempt to balance former overstatements on the particularistic side) to take over the field of prehistory and to make all prehistorians do nomothetic archeology. He does not want to do nomothetic archeology because he takes it to be concerned only with general cultural process and theoretical formulations, whereas he is interested in studying and trying to explain the particular events and processes preserved in the archeological record. We maintain that the only possible separation between generalizing and particularizing processes in the acquisition of knowledge is one of emphasis, for they necessarily operate interdependently.

Because any scientific discipline logically requires both nomothetic and ideographic emphases, and because very few individuals are equally comfortable with and skilled at both, those who are primarily workers in the nomothetic aspects of archeology are as essential as those working primarily from an ideographic orientation and vice-versa. They are complementary, not conflicting, workers. Beyond this necessary complementarity, however, in the practical everyday world of real digging which destroys as it goes, there are reasons why the two emphases are often regarded as (and are) antithetical. That is, an archeologist interested primarily in formulating and testing general laws may ignore data (not reporting them, or, worse, destroying them) that the archeologist interested in detailed historical description would find most important. On the other hand, the ideographically oriented archeologist interested in historical description and reconstruction may report some artifact categories in great detail (for instance, pottery or architecture) but will not even regard as archeological data information vital to a particular theoretical formulation of the nomothetically oriented archeologist (for instance, what is the quantity and context of bitumen waste or chipped stone debris at the site?). How difficult it is to strike a fair balance even when one consciously intends to do so is shown by the discussion of Smith's review of Hole et al. in Chapter 5 above (pp. 157–58).

Similar conflicts are present in other fields; they are not unique to archeology and anthropology, but are particularly acute when, as is the case with anthropological archeology, the field lacks a broad consensus concerning the proper goals of research and of the proper methods to attain them. We have devoted so much space to Trigger's article, because it is an important and honest attempt to speak to an absolutely fundamental issue that must be resolved before anthropological archeologists can come to terms with the forging of such a consensus. That issue, of course, is the objective of archeological research. If we can all agree that one important goal is explanation of particular events and processes in the past, then we must agree first on what we mean by explanation. If we agree that explanation means subsumption of the particular events and processes under appropriate general or covering laws, then we must agree on the source of these laws: Do the necessary confirmed laws already exist, or must we formulate and test them? If the former, what are they? If the latter, how do we go about it? Can we use the archeological record to help us formulate and to test hypothetical laws about particular events in human prehistory and processual aspects of human behavior, and about major aspects of culture and cultural processes? Yes, of course, to the extent that archeology is pursued as a science.

This book begins with the assumption that, logically speaking, scientific archeology is a viable discipline whose practitioners are primarily concerned with explanation of past events and processes, and also with the use of those particular events and processes to help formulate and test culture processual laws. We then present what we believe to be the most important logical and methodological implications of this assumption. By so doing we hope to provide not only a text and guide to scientific archeology but also an organizing framework within which to focus discussion and debate on the issues most crucial to the working out of a conceptual framework for scientific archeology. It is important to recognize, however, that the foundations for such a framework have already been laid by archeologists such as Sir Mortimer Wheeler, who established basic standards of excavation and recording technique; Walter W. Taylor, who stressed the importance of the cultural context of archeological materials; Robert J. Braidwood, who assembled and took to the field the first of the modern, large-scale, interdisciplinary archeological expeditions; and Albert C. Spaulding, who urged the explicit use of scientific method and the adoption of efficient, standardized statistical techniques by archeologists. It is now the task of all of us to come to grips with, and to resolve to our mutual satisfaction, the fundamental questions concerning objectives and goals of our discipline, and to build on the existing foundations a methodological structure enabling us to attain those objectives.

REFERENCES

Aberle, D.
1960   "The Influence of Linguistics on Early Culture and Personality
        Theory," in G. Dole and R. Carneiro, eds., *Essays in the Science
        of Culture in Honor of Leslie A. White*. New York, Thomas Y.
        Crowell Co., 1–29.

Adams, Robert McC.
1966   *The Evolution of Urban Society; early Mesopotamia and pre-
        historic Mexico*. Chicago, Aldine Publishing Company.
1968   "Archeological Research Strategies: Past and Present," *Science*.
        160: 1187–92.

Adams, Robert McC., and H. Nissen
In Press   *The Uruk Countryside*. Chicago, University of Chicago Press.

Anderson, K. M.
1969   "Ethnographic Analogy and Archeological Interpretation," *Sci-
        ence*. 163: 133–38.

Ascher, Robert
1961   "Analogy in Archaeological Interpretation," *Southwestern
        Journal of Anthropology*. 17: 317–25.
1962   "Ethnography for archeology: a case from the Serai Indians,"
        Ethnology. 1: 360–69.

Ashby, W. Ross
1956   *An Introduction to Cybernetics*. New York, John Wiley &
        Sons, Inc.
1962   "Principles of the Self-Organizing System," in Heinz von Foers-
        ter and George W. Zopf, eds., *Principles of Self-Organization*.
        New York, Pergamon Press, Inc., 255–78.

Barth, Fredrik
1956   "Ecologic Relationships of Ethnic Groups in Swat, North Pak-
        istan," *American Anthropologist*. 58: 1079–89.
1961   *Nomads of South Persia: the Basseri tribe of the Khamseh
        confederacy*. Oslo, Oslo University Press.

Bates, Marston
    1953   "Human Ecology," in A. L. Kroeber, ed., *Anthropology
            Today*. Chicago, University of Chicago Press.
Beardsley, R. K. et al.
    1956   "Functional and Evolutionary Implications of Community Pat-
            terning," *Memoirs of the Society for American Archaeology*,
            XI, 129–57.
Bennett, John W.
    1943   "Recent Developments in the Functional Interpretation of Ar-
            cheological Data," *American Antiquity*. 9: 208–19.
Berry, B. J. L.
    1967   *Geography of Market Centers and Retail Distribution*. Engle-
            wood Cliffs, N.J., Prentice-Hall, Inc.
Berry, B. J. L., and A. Baker
    1968   "Geographic Sampling," in B. J. L. Berry and D. Marble, eds.,
            Spatial Analysis. Englewood Cliffs, N.J., Prentice-Hall, Inc.,
            91–100.
Bertalanffy, Ludwig von
    1950   "The Theory of Open Systems in Physics and Biology," *Sci-
            ence*. 111: 23–29.
    1962   "General System Theory—a Critical Review," *General Sys-
            tems*. 7: 1–20.
Binford, Lewis R.
    1962   "Archaeology as Anthropology," *American Antiquity*. 28:
            217–25.
    1964   "A Consideration of Archaeological Research Design," *Ameri-
            can Antiquity*. 29: 425–41.
    1965   "Archaeological Systematics and the Study of Cultural Pro-
            cess," *American Antiquity*. 31: 203–10.
    1967a   "Smudge Pits and Hide-Smoking: the Use of Analogy in Ar-
            chaeological Reasoning," *American Antiquity*. 32: 1–12.
    1967b   Comment on "Major Aspects of the Interrelationship of
            Archaeology and Ethnology," by K. C. Chang, in *Current An-
            thropology*. 8: 234–35.
    1968a   "Archeological Perspectives," in S. Binford and L. Binford,
            eds., *New Perspectives in Archeology*. Chicago, Aldine Pub-
            lishing Company, 5–32.
    1968b   "Post-Pleistocene Adaptations," in S. Binford and L. Binford,
            eds., *New Perspectives in Archeology*. Chicago, Aldine Pub-
            lishing Company, 313–41.
    1968c   "Some Comments on Historical versus Processual Archeology,"
            Southwestern Journal of Anthropology. 24: 267–75.
    1968d   "Methodological Considerations of the Archeological Use of
            Ethnographic Data," in Richard B. Lee and I. DeVore, eds.,

Man the Hunter. Chicago, Aldine Publishing Company, 268–73.

Binford, Lewis R., and Sally R. Binford
1966   "A Preliminary Analysis of Functional Variability in the Mousterian of Levallois Facies," in J. Desmond Clark and F. C. Howell, eds., *Recent Studies in Paleoanthropology; American Anthropologist.* 68, No. 2, Part 2: 238–95.

Binford, Sally R., and Lewis R. Binford, eds.
1968   *New Perspectives in Archeology.* Chicago, Aldine Publishing Company.

Blalock, Hubert M.
1960   *Social Statistics.* New York, McGraw-Hill Book Company.

Boulding, Kenneth
1956   "General Systems Theory—The Skeleton of Science," *Management Science.* 2: 197–208.

Braidwood, Robert J.
1937   *Mounds in the Plain of Antioch: an Archeological Survey.* Oriental Institute Publications, No. 48. Chicago, University of Chicago Press.
1960   "The Agricultural Revolution," *Scientific American.* 203: 130–48.
1967   "Archeology: an introduction," *Encyclopedia Britannica.* 2: 225–27.

Braidwood, R. J., and Bruce Howe et al.
1960   *Prehistoric Investigations in Iraqi Kurdistan.* Studies in Ancient Oriental Civilization, No. 31. Chicago, University of Chicago Press.

Brew, J. O.
1946   *The Archeology of Alkali Ridge, Southeastern Utah.* Papers of the Peabody Museum of American Archeology and Ethnology. Vol. 21. Cambridge, Mass., Harvard University.

Brownlee, K. A.
1965   *Statistical Theory and Methodology in Science and Engineering.* 2nd ed. New York, John Wiley & Sons, Inc.

Buckley, Walter
1967   *Sociology and Modern Systems Theory.* Englewood Cliffs, N.J., Prentice-Hall, Inc.
1968   "Society as a Complex Adaptive System," in Walter Buckley, ed., *Modern Systems Research for the Behavioral Scientist.* Chicago, Aldine Publishing Company, 490–513.

Buckley, Walter, ed.
1968   *Modern Systems Research for the Behavioral Scientist.* Chicago, Aldine Publishing Company.

Byers, D. S., ed.
1967   *The Prehistory of the Tehuacán Valley: Vol. 1. Environment and Subsistence.* Austin, University of Texas Press.

Caldwell, J. R.
1964   "Interaction Spheres in Prehistory," in J. R. Caldwell and R. L. Hall, eds., *Hopewellian Studies.* Illinois State Museum Scientific Papers. 12: 135–43.

Cannon, Walter B.
1939   *The Wisdom of the Body.* New York, W. W. Norton & Company, Inc.

Cattell, R.
1965   "Factor Analysis: An Introduction to Essentials," *Biometrics.* 21: 190–215.

Chang, K. C.
1967   "Major Aspects of the Interrelationship of Archaeology and Ethnology," *Current Anthropology.* 8: 227–34.

Childe, V. Gordon
1937   *Man Makes Himself.* London, Watts and Company.
1942   *What Happened in History.* Harmondsworth, Middlesex, Penguin Books (Pelican A 108).

Clark, J. Desmond
1969   *Kalambo Falls Prehistoric Site.* Vol. I. Cambridge, Cambridge University Press.

Clark, John Grahame D.
1952   *Prehistoric Europe: the Economic Basis.* London, Methuen and Company.
1954   *Excavations at Star Carr; an Early Mesolithic Site at Seamer near Scarborough, Yorkshire.* Cambridge, Cambridge University Press.

Clark, P., and F. Evans
1954   "Distance to Nearest Neighbor as a Measure of Spatial Relationships in Populations," *Ecology.* 35: 445–53.

Clarke, David L.
1968   *Analytical Archaeology.* London, Methuen and Company.

Coe, Michael D., and Kent V. Flannery
1964   "Microenvironments and Mesoamerican Prehistory," *Science.* 143: 650–54.

Cole, J., and C. King
1968   *Quantitative Geography.* New York, John Wiley & Sons, Inc.

Cowgill, George L.
1968   "Archaeological Applications of Factor, Cluster, and Proximity Analysis," *American Antiquity.* 33: 367–75.

Cronin, Constance
1962   "An Analysis of Pottery Design Elements, Indicating Possible Relationships between Three Decorated Types," in Paul S.

Martin, John B. Rinaldo, William A. Longacre, Constance Cronin, Leslie G. Freeman, Jr., and James Schoenwetter. Chapters in the Prehistory of Eastern Arizona, I. Chicago Natural History Museum. *Fieldiana, Anthropology.* 53: 105–14.

Daniels, Steve
1967   "Statistics, Typology and Cultural Dynamics in the Transvaal Middle Stone Age," *South African Archaeological Bulletin.* 22: 114–25.

Deetz, James
1960   An Archaeological Approach to Kinship Change in Eighteenth Century Arikara Culture. Unpublished Ph.D. dissertation, Cambridge, Mass., Harvard University.

1965   *The Dynamics of Stylistic Change in Arikara Ceramics.* Illinois Studies in Anthropology, No. 4. Urbana, Ill., University of Illinois Press.

1967   *Invitation to Archaeology.* Garden City, N.Y., American Museum of Natural History, Natural History Press.

Deetz, James, and E. Dethlefsen
1965   "The Doppler Effect and Archaeology: A Consideration of the Spatial Aspects of Seriation," *Southwestern Journal of Anthropology.* 21: 196–206.

Deming, William E.
1950   *Some Theory of Sampling.* New York, John Wiley & Sons, Inc.

Dethlefsen, E., and James Deetz
1966   "Death's Heads, Cherubs and Willow Trees: Experimental Archaeology in Colonial Cemeteries," *American Antiquity.* 31: 502–10.

Doran, J. P.
1970   "Systems Theory, Computer Simulations and Archaeology," *World Archaeology.* I, No. 3, pp. 289–98.

Downie, N. M., and R. W. Heath
1965   *Basic Statistical Methods.* New York, Harper and Row, Publishers.

Feigl, Herbert, and May Brodbeck, eds.
1953   *Readings in the Philosophy of Science.* New York, Appleton-Century-Crofts.

Flannery, Kent V.
1965   "The Ecology of Early Food Production in Mesopotamia," *Science.* 147: 1247–56.

1967   "Culture History v. Culture Process: A Debate in American Archaeology," *Scientific American.* 217, No. 2: 119–22.

1968   "Archeological Systems Theory and Early Mesoamerica," in B. Meggers, ed., *Anthropological Archeology in the Americas.* Anthropological Society of Washington, 67–87.

1969   "Origins and Ecological Effects of Early Domestication in Iran and the Near East," in P. Ucko and G. Dimbleby, eds., *The Domestication and Exploitation of Plants and Animals.* London, Duckworth (Chicago, Aldine Publishing Company), 73–100.

Flannery, Kent V., and Michael D. Coe
1968   "Social and Economic Systems in Formative Mesoamerica," in S. Binford and L. Binford, eds., *New Perspectives in Archeology.* Chicago, Aldine Publishing Company, 267–84.

Ford, J. A.
1949   "Cultural Dating of Prehistoric Sites in Virú Valley, Peru," *Anthropological Papers of the American Museum of Natural History.* 43, Part 1: 31–89.
1962   *A Quantitative Method for Deriving Cultural Chronology.* Washington, D.C., Pan American Union, No. 1.

Foster, George
1965   "The Sociology of Pottery: Questions and Hypotheses Arising from Contemporary Mexican Work," in F. Matson, ed., *Ceramics and Man.* Viking Fund Publications in Anthropology, No. 41, 43–61.

Freeman, Leslie G.
1968   "A Theoretical Framework for Interpreting Archeological Materials," in Richard B. Lee and Irven DeVore, eds., *Man the Hunter.* Chicago, Aldine Publishing Company, 262–67.

Freund, John E.
1960   *Modern Elementary Statistics.* Englewood Cliffs, N.J., Prentice-Hall, Inc.

Fritz, John M., and Fred Plog
1970   "The Nature of Archaeological Explanation," *American Antiquity.* 35: 405–12.

Goldschmidt, Walter
1959   *Man's Way; a preface to the understanding of human society.* New York, Holt, Rinehart and Winston, Inc.
1966   *Comparative Functionalism; an essay in anthropological theory.* Berkeley, University of California Press.

Gould, R. A.
1968   "Living Archaeology: the Ngatatjara of Western Australia," *Southwestern Journal of Anthropology.* 24: 101–22.

Haggett, P.
1965   *Locational Analysis in Human Geography.* London, Edward Arnold.

Hall, A. D., and R. E. Fagen
1956   "Definition of System," *General Systems* 1: 18–28.

Harary, Frank, Robert Z. Norman, and Dorwin Cartwright

1965   *Structural Models: an Introduction to the Theory of Directed Graphs.* New York, John Wiley & Sons, Inc.

Harlan, J., and D. Zohary
1966   "Distribution of Wild Wheats and Barley," *Science.* 153: 1074–80.

Harman, H. H.
1967   *Modern Factor Analysis.* Chicago, University of Chicago Press.

Harvey, D.
1969   *Explanation in Geography.* London, Edward Arnold, Ltd.

Heizer, Robert F., and J. A. Graham
1967   *A Guide to Field Methods in Archaeology; approaches to the anthropology of the dead.* Palo Alto, Calif., National Press.

Helm, June
1962   "The Ecological Approach in Anthropology," *American Journal of Sociology.* 67: 630–39.

Hempel, C. G.
1965   *Aspects of Scientific Explanation, and Other Essays in the Philosophy of Science.* New York, The Free Press.
1966   *Philosophy of Natural Science.* Englewood Cliffs, N.J., Prentice-Hall, Inc.

Hempel, C. G., and Paul Oppenheim
1948   "Studies in the Logic of Explanation," *Philosophy of Science.* 15: 135–75.

Hill, James N.
1965   Broken K: a Prehistoric Society in Eastern Arizona. Unpublished Ph.D. dissertation, University of Chicago.
1966   "A Prehistoric Community in Eastern Arizona," *Southwestern Journal of Anthropology.* 22: 9–30.
1968   "Broken K Pueblo: Patterns of Form and Function," in S. Binford and L. Binford, eds., *New Perspectives in Archeology.* Chicago, Aldine Publishing Companv, 103–42.
1970a   "Broken K: a Prehistoric Society in Eastern Arizona," *Anthropological Papers of the University of Arizona.* No. 18. Tucson, Arizona.
1970b   "Prehistoric Social Organization in the American Southwest: Theory and Method," in W. Longacre, ed., *Reconstructing Prehistoric Pueblo Societies.* Albuquerque, University of New Mexico Press, 11–58.

Hoel, Paul G.
1960   *Elementary Statistics.* New York, John Wiley & Sons, Inc.
1962   *Introduction to Mathematical Statistics.* New York, John Wiley & Sons, Inc.

Hole, Frank, Kent V. Flannery, and James A. Neely

1969   *Prehistory and Human Ecology of the Deh Luran Plain; an Early Village Sequence from Khuzistan, Iran.* Memoirs of the Museum of Anthropology, Ann Arbor, University of Michigan, No. 1.

Hole, Frank, and Robert F. Heizer
1969   *An Introduction to Prehistoric Archeology.* 2nd ed. New York, Holt, Rinehart and Winston, Inc.

Huntington, Ellsworth
1945   *Mainsprings of Civilization.* New York, John Wiley & Sons, Inc.

Kerrich, J. E., and David L. Clarke
1967   "Notes on the Possible Misuse and Errors of Cumulative Percentage Frequency Graphs for the Comparison of Prehistoric Artefact Assemblages," *Proceedings of the Prehistoric Society.* 33: 57–69.

King, Leslie J.
1969   *Statistical Analysis in Geography.* Englewood Cliffs, N.J., Prentice-Hall, Inc.

Kolstoe, Ralph H.
1969   *Introduction to Statistics for the Behavioral Sciences.* Homewood, Ill., Dorsey Press.

Kroeber, A. L.
1939   *Cultural and Natural Areas of Native North America.* University of California Publications in American Archaeology and Ethnology. 38: 1–242.

Kuhn, T. S.
1962   *The Structure of Scientific Revolutions.* Paperback edition, 1964. Chicago, University of Chicago Press.

Lattimore, Owen
1962   *Studies in Frontier History: Collected Papers 1928–1958.* London, Oxford University Press.

Leach, Edmond R.
1954   *Political Systems of Highland Burma; a study of Kachin social structure.* Cambridge, Mass., Harvard University Press.

Lee, Richard B.
1968   "What Hunters Do for a Living, or, How to Make Out on Scarce Resources," in Richard B. Lee and Irven DeVore, eds., *Man the Hunter.* Chicago, Aldine Publishing Company, 30–48.

Leone, Mark P.
1968   "Neolithic Economic Autonomy and Social Distance," *Science.* 162: 1150–51.

Longacre, William A.
1963   Archeology as Anthropology: A Case Study. Unpublished Ph.D. dissertation, University of Chicago.

1966   "Changing Patterns of Social Integration: A Prehistoric Exam-
          ple from the American Southwest," *American Anthropologist.*
          68: 94–102.
1968   "Some Aspects of Prehistoric Society in East-Central Arizona,"
          in S. Binford and L. Binford, eds., *New Perspectives in Ar-
          cheology.* Chicago, Aldine Publishing Company, 89–102.
1970   Analysis of Burials from the Grasshopper Ruin, Arizona.
          Paper read at the Thirty-fifth Annual Meeting of the Society
          for American Archeology, Mexico City, May, 1970.

Lumley, Henry de
1969   "A Paleolithic Camp at Nice," *Scientific American.* 220, No. 5:
          42–50.

MacNeish, Richard S.
1964   "Ancient Mesoamerican Civilization," *Science.* 143: 531–37.
1967   "A Summary of the Subsistence," in D. S. Byers, ed., *The Pre-
          history of the Tehuacán Valley: Vol. 1. Environment and Sub-
          sistence.* Austin, University of Texas Press, pp. 290–310.

Martin, Paul S.
1971   "The Revolution in Archaeology," *American Antiquity.* 36:
          1–8.

Maruyama, Magoroh
1963   "The Second Cybernetics: Deviation-Amplifying Mutual
          Causal Processes," *American Scientist.* 51: 164–79.

Meggers, Betty, ed.
1968   *Anthropological Archeology in the Americas.* Washington,
          D.C., The Anthropological Society of Washington.

Moroney, M. J.
1956   *Facts from Figures.* 2nd ed. Baltimore, Penguin Books, Inc.
          (Pelican A 236).

Neumann, John von, and O. Morgenstern
1947   *Theory of Games and Economic Behavior.* 2nd ed. Princeton,
          N.J., Princeton University Press.

Odum, E. P.
1953   *Fundamentals of Ecology.* Philadelphia, W. B. Saunders Com-
          pany.
1963   *Ecology.* New York, Holt, Rinehart, and Winston, Inc.

Piggott, Stuart
1965   *Ancient Europe, from the Beginnings of Agriculture to Classi-
          cal Antiquity; a Survey.* Chicago, Aldine Publishing Company.

Plog, Fred
1968   Archaeological Survey—A New Perspective. Unpublished
          M.A. thesis, University of Chicago.

Ragir, S.
1967   "A Review of Techniques for Archaeological Sampling," in
          Robert F. Heizer and J. A. Graham, eds., *A Guide to Field*

Methods in Archaeology; approaches to the anthropology of the dead. Palo Alto, Calif., National Press, 181–97.

Rapoport, Anatol
1953   "What Is Information?" *ETC.* 10: 247–60.
1956   "The Promise and Pitfalls of Information Theory," *Behavioral Science.* I: 303–309.
1959   "Critiques of Game Theory," *Behavioral Science.* 4: 49–66.
1968   "Forward," in W. Buckley, ed., *Modern Systems Research for the Behavioral Scientist.* Chicago, Aldine Publishing Company, *xiii–xxii.*

Rapoport, Anatol, and W. J. Horvath
1959   "Thoughts on Organization Theory and a Review of Two Conferences," *General Systems.* 4: 87–93.

Redman, Charles L.
1971   Controlled Surface Collection as an Integral Element in Archeological Research Strategies. Unpublished Ph.D. dissertation, University of Chicago.

Redman, Charles L., and Patty Jo Watson
1970   "Systematic, Intensive Surface Collection," *American Antiquity.* 35: 279–91.

Renfrew, Colin
1969   "Trade and Culture Process in European Prehistory," *Current Anthropology.* 10: 151–69.

Rudner, Richard S.
1966   *Philosophy of Social Science.* Englewood Cliffs, N.J., Prentice-Hall, Inc.

Sabloff, Jeremy, and Gordon R. Willey
1967   "The Collapse of Maya Civilization in the Southern Lowlands: a Consideration of History and Process," *Southwestern Journal of Anthropology.* 23: 311–36.

Sackett, James R.
1966   "Quantitative Analysis of Upper Paleolithic Stone Tools," in J. Desmond Clark and F. Howell, eds., *Recent Studies in Paleoanthropology.* American Anthropologist Special Publication. 68, No. 2, Part 2: 356–94.

Sauer, Carl
1930   "Historical Geography and the Western Frontier," in James F. Willard and Colin B. Goodykoontz, eds., *The Trans-Mississippi West.* Boulder, University of Colorado Press, 267–89.
1963   *Land and Life; a selection from the writings of Carl Ortwin Sauer.* Ed. by John Leighly. Berkeley, University of California Press.

Siegel, Sidney
1956   *Nonparametric Statistics for the Behavioral Sciences.* New York, McGraw-Hill Book Company.

Smith, P. E. L.
1970   "Ecological Archeology in Iran," a review of Frank Hole,
         Kent V. Flannery, and James A. Neely, *Prehistory and Human
         Ecology of the Deh Luran Plain. Science.* 168: 707–709.
Spaulding, Albert C.
1953   "Statistical Techniques for the Discovery of Artifact Types,"
         American Antiquity. 18: 305–13.
1954   Reply to Ford, "Comment on A. C. Spaulding, 'Statistical Tech-
         niques for the Discovery of Artifact Types,' " *American An-
         tiquity.* 19: 391–93.
1960   "Statistical Description and Comparison of Artifact Assem-
         blages," in R. F. Heizer and S. F. Cook, eds., *The Application
         of Quantitative Methods in Archaeology.* Viking Fund Publica-
         tions in Anthropology, No. 28, 60–83.
1968   "Explanation in Archeology," in S. Binford and L. Binford,
         eds., *New Perspectives in Archeology.* Chicago, Aldine Pub-
         lishing Company, 33–40.
Steward, Julian H.
1949   "Cultural Causality and Law: A Trial Formulation of the De-
         velopment of Early Civilizations," *American Anthropologist.*
         51: 1–27.
1955   *Theory of Culture Change: the Methodology of Multilinear
         Evolution.* Urbana, Ill., University of Illinois Press.
Steward, J. H., and F. M. Setzler
1938   "Function and Configuration in Archaeology," *American An-
         tiquity.* 4: 4–10.
Struever, Stuart
1968a   "Problems, Methods and Organization: a Disparity in the
         Growth of Archeology," in B. Meggers, ed., *Anthropological
         Archeology in the Americas,* Washington, D.C., Anthropologi-
         cal Society of Washington, 131–51.
1968b   "Woodland Subsistence-Settlement Systems in the Lower Illi-
         nois Valley," in S. Binford and L. Binford, eds., *New Perspec-
         tives in Archeology.* Chicago, Aldine Publishing Company,
         285–312.
1969a   "Introduction," in A. Zawacki and G. Hausfater, *Early Vegeta-
         tion of the Lower Illinois Valley.* Reports of Investigations,
         No. 17, Springfield, Ill., Illinois State Museum.
1969b   Evolution and Subsistence in the Interior-Riverine Area of
         Eastern United States. Paper read at the Sixty-eighth Annual
         Meeting of the American Anthropological Association in New
         Orleans, November, 1969.
1971   "Comments on Archaeological Data Requirements and Re-
         search Strategy," *American Antiquity.* 36: 9–19.
Taylor, Walter W.

1948   *A Study of Archeology.* Memoir No. 69, American Anthropological Association. Reprinted in 1964 and 1967, Carbondale, Ill., Southern Illinois University Press.

Thompson, R. H.
1958   *Modern Yucatecan Pottery Making.* Beloit, Wis., Society for American Archaeology, Memoir No. 15.

Trigger, Bruce G.
1968   *Beyond History: The Methods of Prehistory.* New York, Holt, Rinehart, and Winston, Inc.
1970   "Aims in Prehistoric Archaeology," *Antiquity.* 44: 26–37.

Vayda, A. P.
1969   "Introduction," in A. P. Vayda, ed., *Environment and Cultural Behavior; ecological studies in cultural anthropology.* New York, Natural History Press, *xi–xvi.*

Vayda, A. P., ed.
1969   *Environment and Cultural Behavior; ecological studies in cultural anthropology.* Garden City, N.Y., American Museum Source Books in Anthropology, Natural History Press.

Walker, Helen M., and Joseph Lev
1958   *Elementary Statistical Methods.* Rev. ed. New York, Holt, Rinehart, and Winston, Inc.

Watson, James D.
1968   *The Double Helix; a personal account of the discovery of the structure of DNA.* New York, Atheneum Publishers.

Watson, Patty Jo
1966   "Clues to Iranian Prehistory in Modern Village Life." *Expedition* 8: 9–19.

Watson, Richard A.
1966   "Discussion: Is Geology Different: A Critical Discussion of *The Fabric of Geology.*" *Philosophy of Science.* 33: 172–85.
1969   "Explanation and Prediction in Geology," *Journal of Geology.* 77: 488–94.
N.D.   Inference in Archeology. Paper read at the Thirty-fifth Annual Meeting of the Society for American Archaeology, Mexico City, May, 1970.

Watson, Richard A., and Patty Jo Watson
1969   *Man and Nature: An Anthropological Essay in Human Ecology.* New York, Harcourt Brace & World, Inc.

Whallon, Robert, Jr.
1968   "Investigations of Late Prehistoric Social Organization in New York State," in S. Binford and L. Binford, eds., *New Perspectives in Archeology.* Chicago, Aldine Publishing Company, 223–44.

Wheeler, Sir Mortimer

1954   *Archaeology from the Earth.* Oxford, Clarendon Press (Pelican Books printing 1956).

White, Leslie A.
1949   *The Science of Culture; a study of man and civilization.* New York, Farrar, Straus & Giroux, Inc.
1959   *The Evolution of Culture; the development of civilization to the fall of Rome.* New York, McGraw-Hill Book Company.

Wiener, Norbert
1954   *The Human Use of Human Beings; cybernetics and society.* 2nd ed. Garden City, N.Y., Doubleday & Company, Inc. (Anchor Books A 34).

Willey, Gordon R.
1953   *Prehistoric Settlement Patterns in the Virú Valley, Peru.* Washington, D.C., Smithsonian Institution, Bureau of American Ethnology, Bulletin 155.
1956   *Prehistoric Settlement Patterns in the New World.* Viking Fund Publications in Anthropology, No. 23. New York, Wenner-Gren Foundation for Anthropological Research.

Willey, Gordon R., and Philip Phillips
1958   *Method and Theory in American Archaeology.* Chicago, University of Chicago Press.

Williams, B. J.
1968   "Establishing Cultural Heterogeneities in Settlement Patterns: an Ethnographic Example," in S. Binford and L. Binford, eds., *New Perspectives in Archeology.* Chicago, Aldine Publishing Company, 161–70.

Wilmsen, Edwin N.
1968   "Functional Analysis of Flaked Stone Artifacts," *American Antiquity.* 33: 156–61.
1970   "Lithic Analysis and Cultural Inference: A Paleo-Indian Case," *Anthropological Papers of the University of Arizona,* No. 16. Tucson, Arizona.

Winters, Howard
1968   "Value Systems and Trade Cycles of the Late Archaic in the Midwest," in S. Binford and L. Binford, eds., *New Perspectives in Archeology.* Chicago, Aldine Publishing Company, 175–222.

Wright, Gary
1969   *Obsidian Analyses and Prehistoric Near Eastern Trade: 7500 to 3500 B.C.* Anthropological Papers No. 37. Ann Arbor, Museum of Anthropology, University of Michigan.

Wright, H.
1969   Interregional Exchange and the Development of Early Mesopotamian Towns. Paper read at the Sixty-eighth Annual Meet-

ing of the American Anthropological Society, New Orleans, November, 1969.

Wright, H. E., Jr.
1968   "Natural Environment of Early Food Production North of Mesopotamia," *Science.* 161: 334–39.

Yates, Frank
1953   *Sampling Methods for Censuses and Surveys.* London, Charles Griffin and Company.

INDEX

Aberle, D., 63
Activity area, 37, 117, 119
Adams, Robert McC., xi, 102, 118
Anderson, K. M., 50
Archeological record, 21, 22, 24, 25, 30, 31, 33, 63, 111-14, 162, 169
Archeological reports, 156-59
Archeology, anthropological, viii, ix, xi-xiii, 161, 171; as art history, ix, 160, 161n; classical, ix; humanistically oriented, ix; new, x, 29, 30, 32, 51, 85, 89, 165; historically oriented, xii, 29, 165; future of, 153-55; as a social science, 159-63; theory, 163-65; nomothetic, 169 ff.
Archives of Archaeology, 158
Ascher, Robert, 49, 51
Ashby, W. Ross, 65, 68, 70
Attributes, 37, 38, 55, 126 ff., 138-39
Axiomatization, 163

Baker, A., 123
Barth, Frederik, 94, 95
Bates, Marston, 88, 89
Beardsley, R. K., 93
Bennett, John W., 159

Berry, B. J. L., 103, 123
Bertalanffy, Ludwig von, 65, 68
Binford, Lewis R., 3, 20-26, 28, 29, 31, 32, 49, 61, 63, 64, 84, 94, 99, 100, 105, 106, 112, 113, 148
Binford, Sally R., 24, 25, 148
Blalock, Hubert M., 135
Boulding, Kenneth, 65, 66
Braidwood, Robert J., 89, 90, 100, 101, 104, 106, 153, 154, 162, 172
Brew, J. O., 126, 127
Brodbeck, May, 3, 5
Broken K Pueblo, 37-45, 133
Brownlee, K. A., 135
Buckley, Walter, 66, 68, 70-73, 75, 87

Caldwell, J. R., 100
Cannon, Walter B., 91
Carter Ranch Pueblo, 34-37, 54, 162
Cartwright, Dorwin, 76
Central place theory, 103
Chang, K. C., 49
Chi-Squared Test, 38, 141, 142, 144, 147
Childe, V. Gordon, 104